T0384628

OPINIONS OF THE PRESS

"A complete description of Latin sounds, an authoritative statement of the classical pronunciation of the Latin word and sentence, an adequate discussion of the still uncertain question of accent, and a very real help to the correct reading of Latin prose and Latin poetry."   *Latin School Journal.*

"This book should be read and kept for reference by all teachers of Latin. There is hardly an unnecessary line in it: many things are stated that are not generally known, and many more that even the best scholars are only too prone to forget. For instance, who is sure of always pronouncing correctly the following words:—*rosa, ver, urbs, cui, mons, ac, non, rex, pars, orator, pater, mollis*—to take a very few simple and common instances? A greater percentage will fail over *fortuitus, libertas, rudimentum, penuria, securus, solitudo, infelices, elaborare, salutavi, amaverunt, utraque, calefacit, antehac*—if not in quantity, in accent. In his fifteen chapters, Mr Westaway gives us most of what is worth knowing, with plenty of exercises and useful lists, and two and a half pages of bibliography."
Athenaeum.

"An admirable and scholarly volume."   *Guardian.*

"We heartily recommend this book to all classical masters."
Catholic Times.

"If our teachers will only master the simple lessons of this manual, there is no fear that the dark ages of our insular jargon will ever return."   *Cambridge Review.*

"Singularly clear and forceful. . . . those who desire to adopt the new pronunciation could not possibly do better than follow the guidance of this ably written book."   *Record.*

"Practical in its aim, fully detailed in its scope, and admirably lucid in its execution. The sections on the length of syllables, and on the difficult subject of hidden quantities, seem to us particularly well done."   *The Month.*

"The volume forms a really sound introduction to phonetics, and many of its readers will assuredly be tempted to pursue the study of that very important subject for its own sake."
Tablet.

"Mr Westaway has produced a very scholarly and thoroughly accurate manual. He disclaims writing for schoolmasters, but we are sure that any schoolmaster, however much an adept at Latin, will thank Mr Westaway for this useful and practical work which we unreservedly recommend."   *Aberdeen Journal.*

QUANTITY AND ACCENT
IN LATIN

QUANTITY AND ACCENT
IN LATIN

An Introduction to the Reading of Latin aloud

BY

F. W. WESTAWAY

FORMERLY ONE OF H.M. INSPECTORS OF
SECONDARY SCHOOLS

SECOND EDITION

" Quare, quum sit certa quædam uox Romani
generis, urbisque propria, in qua nihil offendi,
nihil displicere, nihil animaduerti possit, nihil
sonare aut olere peregrinum, hanc sequamur."
CICERO

CAMBRIDGE
AT THE UNIVERSITY PRESS
1930

" *Si nimius uideor, seraque coronide longus*
  Esse liber, legito pauca; libellus ero.
Terque quaterque mihi finitur carmine paruo
  Pagina : fac tibi me quam cupis esse breuem."

CAMBRIDGE
UNIVERSITY PRESS

University Printing House, Cambridge CB2 8BS, United Kingdom

Cambridge University Press is part of the University of Cambridge.

It furthers the University's mission by disseminating knowledge in the pursuit of
education, learning and research at the highest international levels of excellence.

www.cambridge.org
Information on this title: www.cambridge.org/9781107432994

First edition 1913
Second edition 1930
First published 1930
First paperback edition 2014

A catalogue record for this publication is available from the British Library

ISBN 978-1-107-43299-4 Paperback

PREFACE
TO THE SECOND EDITION

AT the beginning of the present century, classical teaching had many enemies, some of whom maintained that classics was the last subject to foster a sense of accuracy. Absurd as such criticism was, it had this amount of justification—that the majority of teachers of Latin in those days were slipshod over their quantities. For some years I made a practice of jotting down all false quantities that came my way from persons who had left school, and the first edition of this book owes its origin to the lengthy list thus accumulated. I was then much less concerned with this or that pronunciation than with the accuracy of the Latin in the pronunciation used.

Classical teachers have since found that one great result of the introduction of the restored Roman pronunciation is that learners are compelled to pay attention to quantities. Those of us who have had the advantage of being in contact with teachers and learners during the last twenty years know that with the use of the restored pronunciation the accuracy of spoken Latin has increased to an extent quite unexpected. In at least some, perhaps in all, of the schools where the old pronunciation survives, inaccurate quantities are still very common, and this is probably inevitable.

In some quarters the restored Roman pronunciation is confused with the Italian pronunciation. The two things are entirely different.

Scholars agree that the pronunciation of modern Italian differs almost as much from that of Augustan Latin as the pronunciation of modern English does from Anglo-Saxon. As century succeeds century, new differences are bound to creep in, and in course of time the differences become far-reaching and fundamental.

But, in spite of the great difference between the language of ancient Rome and the living language of modern Italy, there seems always to have been a tendency for the Latin of the Church of Rome to be influenced, in its pronunciation, by the living and changing Italian speech. And since, right down to the Reformation, the great majority of English schools were attached to the monasteries and taught by the monks, Latin in England was until that time pronounced in the Italian fashion. The Italian pronunciation has survived amongst the priests of the Church of Rome, in all countries, down to the present day. It is necessarily acquired by the many priests who actually make their studies in Rome, and is then naturally transmitted by them to their associates and their pupils. It is a Latin pronunciation *sui generis*, but with an intonation inevitably varying with the country where it is spoken. It is quite distinct from the pronunciation now used in our schools.

At the Reformation some of the responsible authorities felt that in schools the Italian pronunciation should be abandoned, but an edict issued in 1542 by the Chancellor of the University of Cambridge (Gardiner, Bishop of Winchester), was directed *against* any change in the old method of pronouncing Latin. Inasmuch, however, as the clergy were no

longer compelled to use the language of the Church of Rome,
Latin gradually came to be pronounced as if it were English.
Of uniformity there was none; of accuracy, very little. The
mischief was probably accentuated by the indolence of
grammar school teachers, and after a time it spread to the
Universities. It spread even unto Eton!

By the beginning of the seventeenth century, Latin pronunciation had become barbarous indeed. In 1608, Scaliger
received at Leyden a visit from an English scholar, and after
listening to his Latin for a full quarter of an hour and finding
it utterly unintelligible, was compelled to bring the interview
to an end by apologising, in perfect good faith, for his inade-
quate knowledge of English.

By this time England had, in fact, adopted a pronunciation
which in some ways quite isolated her from European scholars.
This became so marked that, in 1644, Milton directed that
boys should be taught "to fashion a distinct and clear pronunciation, as near as may be to the Italians, especially in
the vowels." "To smatter Latin with an English mouth is as
ill a hearing as law French."

Nevertheless, Latin seems to have been pronounced in the
English way until after the middle of the nineteenth century.
The reformers set to work seriously some sixty years ago and
finally it was decided, not to re-adopt the Italian pronunciation which is still used in many continental countries, but
to restore the original Roman pronunciation of the Augustan
period, a pronunciation known with very close approximation
to such classical scholars as are experts in phonetics and
phonology. So much progress has been made during the

present century that 95°/₀ of the boys and girls now learning
Latin use the restored pronunciation, and the number now
learning Latin is probably eight or ten times as great as at
the beginning of the century.

It is true that some of the modern Italian vowels differ but
little from the restored Roman vowels, but some of the Italian
consonantal sounds differ widely from the Latin sounds. A few
English Church choirmasters when using Latin words sometimes substitute one or two Italian vowels for English vowels
and sometimes they borrow one Italian consonant, viz., the
soft c (= ch) before e and i. The phonetic advantage of the
latter faint tinge of Italian is not obvious.

One of the principal reasons put forward by the surviving
objectors to the restored Roman pronunciation is that it is
confusing to beginners and adds greatly to their difficulties.
Classical *teachers* know better. Time after time I have seen
a first lesson in Latin given to beginners, have often given
one myself. Half an hour is long enough to teach the ten
main vowel sounds (long and short a, e, i, o, and u), the main
rule for syllabic division, and the two main rules for stress-
accent. At the end of that time the child can pronounce the
words in an easy Latin sentence with tolerable accuracy,
although not understanding the meaning. Other rules of
pronunciation need not be formally taught. They may be
mentioned when necessary in the course of the ordinary
lessons. The pupil's pronunciation is perfected gradually,
almost unconsciously, provided the teacher's own pronunciation is perfect. It is only the indolent teacher who dislikes
the restored pronunciation: it means two or three hours

serious work for himself, and the giving up of one game of golf: is it therefore worth while? Of course any inaccuracies on the part of a teacher will be reflected in the boys and be multiplied a hundredfold. That he knows, and fears.

Another reason, not explicitly admitted, for the minority objection to the restored pronunciation is the necessity for careful attention to quantities. I have never known a teacher of the "English" pronunciation whose quantities were consistently accurate. As far as quantities were concerned, that pronunciation was a law unto itself. There was no sort of uniformity. Teachers even in the same school adopted different usages.

Perhaps the greatest reason *for* the adoption of the reformed pronunciation is that we may be able to appreciate the musical quality of the Latin language, especially Latin verse. That quality is mainly a product of the Latin vowel system. If we replace the pure Latin vowels by the diphthongs and the indeterminate murmurings of modern English, the effect is barbarous indeed, as Milton himself only too well realised. Let an unregenerate Latinist listen to two renderings of a few lines of Horace or Virgil, one in the English and one in the Roman pronunciation. Unless he is tone deaf he will reform at once. Let him ask some educated foreigner who is entirely ignorant of spoken English to read a few lines of Milton or Shakespeare. Can he rationally argue that the effect is any worse than his own rendering of Latin? Latin verse is written to be *read aloud* and is therefore written to suit the genius of the *sounds* of the language. To read Latin poetry with alien sounds is to reduce it to a concatenation of

ululations almost calculated to call up the wraith of the
writer whose masterpiece is being murdered.

The pronunciation question was discussed anew by the
Head Masters' Conference in December, 1926, and, despite
fractious opposition from a few, the acceptance of the restored
pronunciation was re-affirmed by a large majority. The discussion led to a protracted correspondence in the press. As
might be expected, the pronouncements of scholarly Head-
masters, for instance Mr Cary Gilson and Mr Guy Kendall in
The Times, and Mr Roxburgh in *The Spectator*, were wholly
in accord with the Conference decision. But a few easy chair
critics, out of touch with modern scholarship, entered pleas
for the sort of Latin they had learnt half a century ago. I am
afraid I was mischievous enough to make inquiries concerning
the accuracy of the quantities in the Latin usage of two or
three of the critics. To give details would be a little unkind,
but I cannot refrain from quoting from one letter, which
appeared in *The Times* on Dec. 28, 1926, over the signature
of a distinguished Churchman holding high office in a famous
Wessex city :

"In this city the very mention of the subject arouses the
fiercest passions. Only the other day I was speaking with a
clergyman on quite another matter when he introduced the
pronunciation of Latin and bit me severely......We have many
of us suffered under, and all of us laughed at, 'Weany, weedy,
weaky.' But what I want to know is why do the idiots (as
they really seem to me) want us Englishmen to pronounce *c*
as the modern Italians do ? Why in the world should we
poor English folk be asked to say 'chivvy' when we mean

civi? My blood boils (or turns cold—I forget which) when I hear the word thus sung.......To turn *j* into *y* is certainly un-English and un-French ('*Yer*, says I, knowing the language'—I don't think!); but *ch* for *c* is, I really do believe, the Scarlet Limit."

How would the writer of the letter pronounce *uēnī* and *iūrō*? Does he still use Latin texts containing those curious old blunders of the printers, the substitution of an English *v* and *j* for Latin consonantal *u* and *i* respectively? Assuredly he knows that there is no *v* or *j* in Latin. And *who* are the " idiots" who want us to pronounce *c* as the modern Italians do? The only people who pronounce *c* in this way are Catholic priests and a few choirmasters, and Catholic priests would certainly not say " chivvy," for it is highly improbable that they would be guilty of false quantities, and the doubled *v*, if not the *y*, obviously implies a short vowel.

Printers and choirmasters are admittedly very intelligent folk: we are all greatly in their debt. But is it not just a little rash to use their Latinity as the main weapon for attacking principles laid down by the recognised authorities on Classics and classical teaching, viz., the Classical Association, the Head Masters' Conference, and the Board of Education?

That clergyman who bites would be extremely useful to the Head-Master of a certain school *juxta Wyndesoram*.

In the present edition, a few necessary amendments have been made, some of them suggested by the late Professor Sonnenschein, who was good enough to put the first edition under his microscope. And, in response to the expressed wishes of several readers, I have added two new chapters, one on the grouping of words in spoken Latin, and one giving a few original extracts from ancient writers dealing with the difficult question of accent.

"Horace," "Virgil," "Livy," and the like have become such familiar household names to us all that it would be pedantry to attempt to restore the names in their original Latin, and nobody suggests that this should be done.

ASPLEY HEATH,
August 1929.

From the PREFACE *to the First Edition*

THE correspondence in *The Times* during the past year makes it clear that we have still with us a remnant of that older race of classical scholars who were ever clamant to be let alone in their easy-going pronunciation of Latin. Yet it was their custom to pride themselves upon their accuracy, and if anyone in their hearing failed to pronounce such words as *antīquus, amīcus, fortūna,* or *imperātor,* with the accent on the long vowel of the penult, or *tárdĭtas, trépĭdus, érĭmus,* or *párĭēs,* with the accent on the antepenult, the offending person was promptly cast without the pale. They seemed to be curiously unconscious of their own amazing blunders; they would shorten the long vowels in all such words as *sōl, nōn, vōx, nīl, lēx, lēctus*[1]*, rēx, rēctum*; they would lengthen the short vowel in the accented syllable of *nŏta, rŏsa, tŏga, vŏlens, bĕne, dĕus, bŏnus, sŏcius, hĭeme, socĭetas*; they frequently accented the antepenult instead of the penult in *minĭster, facŭltas, libĕrtas, excĕllens*; and so with many other analogous words. And if they made use of the phrases *bŏnā fĭdē* or *sĭnĕ quā nōn, fĭdē* was made to rime with "tidy," and *sĭnĕ* with "briny." Do we not, moreover, still occasionally hear of poor "Smith mine-er" (*mĭnŏr*) being called upon, before he makes another attempt to struggle through a few lines from the "Mete(r)mórphe(r)ses"

[1] That is, the participle of *lĕgō. Lectus,* a couch, is of different origin, and in this case the *e* is very probably short.

(*Metamorphŏses*), to join in singing "dull'sy dome'um" (*dŭlcĕ dŏmŭm*)? And does not the old-time K.C., engrossed as he is with musty "nice-eye pry-us" (*nĭsĭ prĭŭs*) records, still get rid of a troublesome case by putting forward a "nolly prossy-kwy" (*nōllĕ prōsĕquī*)?

The remnant of this old school pleads for a retention of the "old" or "English" pronunciation because, they say, it would save trouble in teaching. Is not the poor British school-boy worried enough already[1]? Let him, then, pronounce Latin as he pronounces English.

Obviously, however, the so-called "English" pronunciation of Latin is, in a measure, a misnomer. If, for instance, we pronounced *fĭdē* and *sĭnĕ* after the English pattern, both words would be monosyllables; and such words as *antĭquus*, *amīcus, castīgo, minĭster, magĭster, libĕrtas, facŭltas, honĕstas, māchĭnă, excĕllens*, would, as regards accent, follow the pronunciation of the analogous English words *antiquated, amicable, castigate, minister, magistrate, liberty, faculty, honesty, machine*, and *excellent*, respectively.

Unfortunately, a considerable proportion even of those who now claim to use the restored pronunciation have adopted the change in a half-hearted and incomplete fashion. Practically all they have done is to make use of the new vowel sounds (more or less), and sometimes of consonantal *i* and *u*. It is a common thing for correct syllable length to receive practically no attention at all; and as for the reading of

[1] The wise schoolmaster does not, of course, worry his pupils with rules about the minutiae of Latin pronunciation. Nevertheless he does make sure that his own pronunciation is accurate. Then he has little trouble.

Latin verse, the old-fashioned English accent-rhythm is almost as much in vogue now as it was twenty years ago.

Although the main object of the book is to deal with quantity and accent, a preliminary discussion on the various Latin speech-sounds seems to be indispensable. The usual method of giving roughly approximate English equivalents to the various Latin vowels and diphthongs is by no means satisfactory, yet no other method is possible unless the reader is prepared to take up the subject of phonetics systematically and thoroughly. If we say that a particular Latin sound is to be uttered in the same way as a particular English sound, do we mean the English sound as heard in London, or in Devonshire, or in Yorkshire, or in Scotland, or in America, or where? Comparatively few English people ever lose completely every trace of their own particular dialect, though perhaps few educated men willingly admit any departure from standard English in their own speech-sounds. But in standard English, there is a recognised position of the organs of speech for every sound uttered. The slightest departure from a particular position is bound to result in a different sound. It is the function of phonetics to determine the exact positions for all sounds. Accuracy can be attained only if the organs of speech are so trained that they can be instantly brought into the exact position necessary for the production of any particular sound. Primarily the whole matter is organic, not merely acoustical.

To deal adequately with such a large subject as phonetics in a book of this size is out of the question. Yet it seems necessary to touch upon the subject to some slight extent, if only to enable the reader to acquire a clear notion of a diphthong and to understand the inner nature of our slovenly English habits of speech. There is probably no nation in Europe which drawls its speech and clips its words as we English do. It is therefore necessary to learn *how* and *where* our speech is slovenly and imperfect, for Latin was almost free from those very imperfections which are so common in English. If due attention is paid to the hints given in the earlier pages of this book, it is believed that the various Latin sounds may be uttered in such a way as to satisfy all scholars except the highly-trained phonetic expert. But the reader must be under no delusion ; absolute accuracy can be attained only from a serious study of phonetic principles. And unless he already speaks standard English, it is hopeless for him to expect to attain even approximate accuracy in Latin.

The pronunciation of Latin at which classical scholars are now aiming is a standard pronunciation, namely, the Latin spoken by educated Romans in the Augustan period. That pre- and post-Augustan Latin differed from this is probably true, but that does not matter.

After a knowledge of the sound values of the various Latin vowels and consonants has been acquired, it is important to obtain correct notions of syllable length, for this is the key to the correct reading of Latin, prose as well as verse. It was the lengthening of short vowels and the shortening of long vowels—mainly the result of regarding accent in Latin as the same as accent in English—that led many classical scholars to read Latin in such a way as to make it entirely unlike the Latin of the Romans.

Hidden quantities have been dealt with in some detail.
It is idle to contend that attention to hidden quantities in-
volves any appreciable additional difficulty in learning Latin.
The first time a learner meets with the word *amīcus,* he sees
the long vowel and knows that he must pronounce it long.
Why, then, should there be any difficulty about such a word
as *nōllĕ?* There is no need to tell the beginner anything
about hidden quantities : that will come later on. All he has
to do is to pronounce all long vowels long. The rules about
the greater number of hidden quantities are few and easily
mastered, and though a learner will probably make occasional
mistakes by bringing in exceptional cases under the rules, his
mistakes will be far fewer than they would be if he ignored
hidden quantities altogether. After all, the undecided cases
of hidden quantity are relatively few.

It is practically certain that the element of doubt still
enshrouding some aspects of the question of hidden quantities
will tend rapidly to pass away, now that scholars are attacking
the question from the point of view of phonetics and phonology. Hitherto, too much reliance has been placed upon analogical and inferential evidence. No doubt this is very helpful,
but much remains to be done in regard to discovering the
precise phonetic laws underlying the speech of the Romans.

Prosody has been only very lightly touched upon, just
sufficiently to put the reader on his guard against imitating
the heavy accent-rhythm characteristic of English poetry.
The subject is a large one, and for general details the reader
must refer to the works of recognised grammarians and
metricians.

In classical research, rival hypotheses, possibly both wrong, certainly not both right, may exist side by side for an indefinite period. The hypotheses of one classical scholar may be adopted as facts by another, a procedure which would be ridiculed in scientific investigation. In analogical reasoning, points of resemblance are not always weighed, but counted. In balancing probabilities and in forming a judgment the necessity for an entire elimination of preconceptions in favour of a particular theory is sometimes forgotten. All these things apply especially to many of those who have made the nature of Latin "accent" a subject of investigation. If ancient testimony clashes with their own deductions, so much the worse for ancient testimony! It is surprising to find what dogmatic statements are made, sometimes in favour of a stress-accent, sometimes in favour of a pitch-accent, although it is notorious that the facts at present available are altogether insufficient to admit of a definite conclusion.

It is therefore satisfactory to find a wise reserve and a cultivated caution exercised by present-day British classical scholars. Of these, Professor Postgate, representing Cambridge, and Professor W. M. Lindsay, representing Oxford, may be singled out specially. The latter's *Latin Language* is universally regarded as an authoritative work of the greatest weight, while the former's numerous scholarly contributions to philology are well known to all who are interested in classical research.

CONTENTS

CHAPTER I

LATIN AND ENGLISH VOWELS

1. ENGLISH spelling is not phonetic. Spelling is said to be phonetic when it indicates exactly the sounds made in speaking, and for this purpose it is necessary

- (*a*) That there should be a symbol for each spoken sound;
- (*b*) That each symbol should stand for only one sound;
- (*c*) That in writing a word no sound should be omitted;
- (*d*) That no unpronounced symbols should be used.

English spelling violates all these rules. Latin, on the other hand, is almost perfectly phonetic; so was Anglo-Saxon. Hence there is little difficulty in learning to pronounce correctly either Latin or Anglo-Saxon.

2. The foundation of speech is breath expelled by the lungs and variously modified in the throat and mouth.

A *vowel*[1] is merely voiced breath emitted through the open mouth channel. Every time we move the tongue and lips we create a new resonance chamber, which moulds the voice into a different vowel. But the possible positions of

---

[1] In the formation of *nasal* vowels, voiced breath flows through the nose as well as through the mouth.

the tongue and lips are infinite; it therefore follows that the number of possible vowel sounds is infinite. No wonder, then, that we have such a large number of different vowels in different languages.

3. The difficulty in understanding English vowel sounds is chiefly due to the unfortunate names we give to the symbols *a, e, i, o,* and *u.* The names of all five symbols are really diphthongs, and are therefore misleading. The same symbols in Latin represent pure vowels.

But even in Latin each of the five symbols *a, e, i, o,* and *u* has to represent two sounds, these being usually distinguished as *long* and *short*; for instance, we have long *a* (written ā) and short *a* (written ă). But these terms long and short are not wholly adequate, for while there is always a difference of *time* there is usually also a further difference of *quality.*

4. To understand these differences, it is necessary to learn to isolate a particular sound from any given word containing it.

(*a*) Isolate the vowel sound *a* in the word *father.* To do this, first pronounce the whole word, then cut off the final syllable -*ther,* and afterwards the *f.* Keep the mouth open, prolong the vowel sound, and carefully note, by means of a mirror, the position of the tongue. Note also the muscular sensation, in order that the same position may be recognised again.

Now, without in any way changing the position of the tongue, *shorten* the vowel sound. The sound is exactly the same as before, except as regards the *time* taken to pronounce it. The *quality* of the sound is the same. If, however, there is the slightest alteration in the tongue position, or indeed in any part of the mouth or throat, some different vowel sound will result.

This short *a* sound is really extinct in modern English, though it is very nearly heard in the second syllable of the word *grandfather*, and in the first syllable of *aha*. The sound of *a* in the word *man* is not of the same *quality* as the short *a* in question.

The long *a* sound in the word *father* and in the second syllable of *aha* is the Latin long *a*; the short *a* sound in the second syllable of *grandfather* and in the first syllable of *aha* is, as nearly as possible, the Latin short *a*.

(*b*) Isolate the short vowel sound in the word *fit*, first pronouncing the whole word, then cutting off the *t*, and then the *f*. Now try to lengthen the sound without allowing it to pass into the *i* sound in the word *machine*. The tongue should remain quite *lax*. If it becomes tense or taut, the sound in *machine* will result, and this is not only a *longer* sound as regards time, but is different in *quality*.

Now utter the two sounds, the short *i* in *fit*, and the long *i* in *machine*, alternately. Watch the change in the tongue position, and note the respective muscular sensations. In the case of the short *i*, the tongue lies easy and *relaxed*; it is thin and *wide*, and " wide " is the term used to describe such a sound. In the case of the long *i*, the surface of the tongue becomes more convex and there is a marked feeling of *tenseness*. The tongue is bunched up and *narrow*, and " narrow " is the term used to describe such a sound.

(c) Isolate the long vowels in the words *fate, note,* and *brute.* Note the tense feeling of the tongue in each case. The vowels are narrow.

Isolate the short vowels in the words *sped, not,* and *pull.* Note the easy relaxed feeling of the tongue. The vowels are wide.

(d) Isolate the *o* sounds in the words *obey* and *note.* There is a difference of length only. There is no difference of quality. With these, compare the two *a* sounds and the two *i* sounds already described.

(e) Isolate the long narrow *o* sound in the word *note,* and prolong it. As the sound ceases, an "easing down" of the tense feeling of the tongue may be detected. The pure *o* sound is thus not cut off promptly. The unconscious alteration of position produces an alteration of sound, and the pure *o* sound is followed by an easily perceptible secondary sound[1]. The English long *o* is therefore really a diphthong, though the second element is slight. The secondary and final sound is a *u* sound, and is very distinct when it comes at the end of a word as in *no.* It is scarcely heard in such a word as *noble.* Cut off this secondary sound and we have the pure vowel sound heard in the German word *Sohn.* This is the Latin long *o.*

(f) Isolate the long vowel sound in the word *fate.* Note its diphthongal nature, due to a secondary and final *i* sound. The secondary sound is scarcely heard in such a word as *nation.* Cut off the secondary sound, and we have the pure vowel sound heard in the German word *fehlen.* This is the Latin long *e.*

---

[1] Cf. §§ 13 and 14 in the next chapter.

(g) Isolate the long *i* sound in the word *machine*. Note its diphthongal nature, due to a secondary and final *y* sound. Cut off the secondary sound and we have the pure vowel sound heard in the German *ihn* or French *livre*. This is the Latin long *i*.

(h) Isolate the vowel sound in the word *brute*. Note its diphthongal nature due to the secondary and final *w* sound. Cut off the secondary sound and we have the pure vowel sound heard in German *du* or French *rouge*. This is the Latin long *u*.

5. It will now be clear that the English names we give to the symbols *a* (as in *fate*), *e* (as in *machine* or *seen*), and *o* (as in *note*), are not pure vowels; they are diphthongs. The English names we give to the symbols *i* (as in *pine*), and *u* (as in *duke*), are referred to in § 14.

Even the sound of *a* in *father* is possibly slightly diphthongal, but the secondary and final sound is so slight as almost to be imperceptible, and is in consequence difficult to analyse.

6. The Latin short vowels, *ă*, *ĕ*, *ĭ*, *ŏ* and *ŭ*, are easy to pronounce. They are heard respectively in the English words *grandfather* (second syllable)[1], *sped*, *fit*, *not*, and *pull*.

There is some difference of opinion about Latin short *o*. Some authorities consider it to be merely the shortened form of the long *o* (as in *obey* or *democrat*), but the weight of opinion is in favour of the *o* sound in *not*.

7. The only new vowel sound to be learned in Latin is the *y* found in certain words borrowed from the Greek. It

---

[1] But see last paragraph of § 4 (*a*).

is really the French *u*, or German *ü*. The sound results from a combination of the tongue articulation of the *i* sound and the lip-rounding of the *u* sound.

(*a*)   Isolate the vowel sound in the word *brute*, and very carefully observe the rounding of the lips.

(*b*)   Now isolate the long *i* sound in the word *machine*. Note the exact position of the tongue and retain that position. Now round the lips as for the *u* sound in *brute*, and again utter the long *i* sound. The vowel sound in French *ruse* or German *Güte* results. This is Latin long *y* (*ȳ*).

(*c*)   Now do the same with the short vowel sound *i* in the word *fit*. The vowel sound in German *Sünde* results. This is very nearly, but not quite, Latin short *y* (*y̆*). The *quality* of the Latin *y̆* is the same as the Latin *ȳ*; the difference is a difference of *length* only. Latin *y̆* is almost exactly heard in French *cultiver*, where we have the same "narrow," "tense" sound, but shorter, as in French *ruse*. Perhaps the sound is best obtained by isolating the *u* in French *ruse* and then shortening it, but in the shortening the tongue must be kept tense. As in French *ruse* and *cultiver*, so with Latin *ȳ* and *y̆* (really Greek *ῡ* and *ῠ*); the *quality* of the sound is the same.

8.   In certain Latin words the spelling varies between *i* and *u*, for instance, **maximus** and **maxumus**, **optimus** and **optumus**, and there is little doubt that in these cases the actual vowel sound heard was intermediate between *i* and *u*, and practically equivalent to Latin *y̆*, as in German *Sünde* see above. It was a lax, not a tense sound, and

therefore not quite the same as Greek *v*. The Latin *y̆*
sound, rendered lax, should be adopted for such words.

9. Latin short vowels, when final, are very seldom
pronounced correctly. For final short *a* (as in **vīllă**) the
tendency is to substitute the vague and indefinite sound
heard at the end of the English word china. For final *ĕ*
and *ĭ* the tendency is to substitute the short sound heard
at the end of the English words *lady, sorry*; thus, **possĕ**
is often pronounced as *possy*, and **nĭsĭ** as *nissy*. For final
ŏ, *ō* is often substituted; thus **mŏdŏ** is pronounced *mŏdō*
(or even *mōdō*). These are serious faults.

The best way to obtain the correct pronunciation is first
to pronounce the word with an added *t*[1] at the end. Thus,
first pronounce the .imaginary words *vīllăt, possĕt, nĭsĭt,
mŏdŏt*, distinctly; then cut off the *t*, and preserve the
accurate pronunciation of the final short vowel. Except
for the different position of the break at the end of the
word, **parcĕ tĭbĭ** and **parcĕt ĭbĭ**, **rĕgĕrĕ tĕstĭs** and **rĕgĕrĕt
ĕstĭs** are pronounced exactly alike. In such a word as
hĭĕmĕ it is best first to pronounce correctly the imaginary
form **hĭtĕmĕt**; then omit the two *t*'s and carefully preserve
the vowel sounds.

10. The following table includes the twelve Latin vowel
sounds already discussed. Words from English, French, and
German are given to illustrate the sounds, but the words in
brackets give the sounds only approximately. The references
are, of course, to *standard* English, French, and German[2].

---

[1] One of the best letters. Some letters would be misleading, for instance
the letter *r*. For the reason of this, see any text-book on phonetics.

[2] This table is as accurate as it can be made for those unfamiliar with

Latin vowel	Illustrative Latin words	The same sound in examples from standard			Phonetic symbol
		English	French	German	
ā	ărās, intrā, māllem	father	âme	Vater	a:
ă	ămăt, dăre, mēnsă	grandfather	[pas]	was	a
ē	tēlă, mēnsă, dīē	[fate]	[église]	fehlen	e:
ĕ	tĕnĕt, rĕgĕrĕ, implĕās	sped	[avec]	fett	ɛ
ī	ībam, īnfēnsŭs, fīĕrī	[machine]	livre	ihn	l:
ĭ	sĭtĭs, ĭēns, nĭsĭ	fit	[vif]	mit	l
ō	mōs, mōtĭō, cōnsŭl	[noble]	chaud	Sohn	o:
ŏ	bŏnŭs, mŏdŏ, ĕgŏ	not	[robe]	Sonne	ɔ
ū	ūtĭlĭs, tūnsŭs, gĕnū	[brute]	rouge	du	ú:
ŭ	tŭŭs, fĭŭnt, ŭxŏr	pull	[nouvelle]	und	ù
ȳ[1]	gȳrūs, Hȳlēs, Massȳle	—	ruse	Güte	y:
ў[1]	cўmbă, Hўădēs, Sўphāx	—	cultiver	[Sünde]	y

11.   Note that

Latin ā is never like English *a* in *fate*.

    „   ē   „   „   „   *e* „ *scene*.

    „   ī   „   „   „   *i* „ *pine*.

    „   ū   „   „   „   *u* „ *duke*.

    „   ŭ   „   „   „   *u* „ *nut*.

phonetics. Most of the bracketed words contain the sounds very approximately, but the trained ear of the phonetician easily detects shades of difference. For instance, nearly all French vowels are of the "narrow," "tense" variety; they are not "wide," "relaxed," as in the case of the short English and German vowels. The French *é* sound really differs substantially from Lat. ē; it is much shorter. Even in the unbracketed words the parallelism is not in all cases absolutely exact. The *a* sound in French *âme*, for example, is not quite identical with that in English *father* or German *Vater*.

¹ In Greek-borrowed words only.

CHAPTER II

LATIN AND ENGLISH DIPHTHONGS

12. Latin diphthongs are seldom pronounced correctly, but the pronunciation is easily mastered, once the nature of a diphthong is understood.

13. A *glide* is a transitional sound, generally used unconsciously, produced during the transition from one sound to the other. Pronounce the word *key* : here we have the initial consonant (a back position) sound, and the final vowel (a front position) sound. The glide is the sound produced in passing from one to the other. With a little practice, the muscular movement in the production of the glide may be detected.

To the student of phonetics, glides are of great importance, but it will suffice here if the reader can distinguish clearly between the initial and the final element of a diphthongal vowel sound.

14. We have seen that when, in pronouncing the vowel sound in such a word as *no*, the sound ceases, there is an unconscious alteration of position, a final and secondary sound being produced.

But there may be a *conscious* change from one vowel position to another. In such a case, the initial and final vowels, with the vowel glide between them, constitute a diphthong. Each of the two vowels virtually loses its own "syllabicness"; the vocal organs shift rapidly from one position to the other, and there is combination of sound, though one of the vowels takes the chief stress.—A little practice with a few English diphthongs will make this clear.

(*a*) Isolate and pronounce in succession the Latin short vowel sounds *ă* and *ĭ*, first slowly, and then more rapidly, until the two coalesce and form the diphthong *ai*. Note how the *a* is stressed, and how weak the *i* in the combination becomes. The combined sound is the name we give to the English letter *i*, that is the vowel sound heard in the word *pine*. (Do not be misled by the combination *ai* in such a word as *maid*, which is quite a different sound.)

Clearly, then, the name we give to the English letter *i* is a diphthong.

(*b*) Now resolve this diphthong, that is the vowel sound heard in the word *pine*, into its elements, uttering the diphthong first in the ordinary way, then more and more slowly until the separate *a* and *i* sounds are detected. (Note: if the element *a* be lengthened to the long *a* in the word *father*, and the diphthong be reconstituted, the cockney pronunciation of the *i* sound in *pine* will result.)

(*c*) Resolve the diphthong *ou* in the English word *loud* into its elements. They are, respectively, Latin *ā* and *ŭ*. (Note: if the Latin *ā* be shortened to Latin *ă*, and the diphthong be reconstituted, the cockney pronunciation of *ou* will result; for instance, in the word *house*.) (Cf. § 16 *b*.)

(*d*) Resolve the diphthong *oi* in the English word *moist* into its elements; they are, respectively, Latin *ŏ* and *ĭ*.

(*e*) Resolve the diphthong *u* in the English word *duke* into its elements; they are, respectively, Latin *ĭ* and *ū*. This diphthong is the name we give to the English letter *u*.

15. Not one of these four diphthongs occurs in Latin, but the reader ought now to be able to pronounce those that do so occur. They are six in number. Three of them, viz., **ae, au, oe,** are common; the other three, viz., **ei, eu, ui,** are rare.

16. The six Latin diphthongs have no exact equivalents in English, and their pronunciation must be learnt by first sounding each Latin vowel separately, and then running them together. If attention be paid to the suggestions in the preceding section, there should be no difficulty in effecting the fusion accurately.

The following remarks may be helpful:

(*a*) Lat. **ae** (as in t**ae**dae) may be pronounced as in *Isaiah*[1] when pronounced broadly. Fr. *travail* gives the sound fairly accurately if the final vanishing sound of the liquid be omitted. The sound is never like *ai* in Eng. *maid*, or *ee* in Eng. *feed*.[2]

(*b*) Lat. **au** (as in l**au**do) is the *ou* of Eng. *house* broadly pronounced, though not quite so broad as in the cockney pronunciation. Ger. *Haus* (containing more of the *u* sound than Eng. *house*) gives the Latin sound exactly. But it is not certain that Lat. **au** is **ā + u** in

---

[1] Old Latin *ai* was, as Professor Postgate points out, certainly pronounced as in *Isaiah*, but when *ai* was changed to *ae* there was probably a change in the sound of the second element from *i* to *e*. So with *oe* (*oi*).

[2] It is not quite like Ger. *ä* which is a pure vowel and not a diphthong.

all cases. It may sometimes have been ă + u. The
Latin sound **au** is never like *au* in Eng. *fraud* or in
Fr. *pauvre*.

(*c*) Lat. **oe** (as in **foe**dus) is something like *oi* in
Eng. *boil*; the *äu* in Ger. *Häuser* is also an approximation. It is never like *ee* in Eng. *feed.*

(*d*) Lat. **ei** is something like *ei* in Eng. *rein* or *ey*
in *grey*. It is a diphthong in h**ei** and Pomp**ei** (voc.).
But the combination **ei** is far more common in separate
syllables, e.g. **dĭēī, fĭdĕī**. The nature of the **ei** in
deinde is not quite free from doubt. In classical verse
the word is always disyllabic, and there appears to be
no good reason to think that it was differently pronounced in prose.

(*e*) Lat. **eu** (as in n**eu**ter) is very nearly like the
ou in the cockney pronunciation of Eng. *house*. It is
never like *eu* in Eng. *feud*. Lat. **heu** is very much
like the cockney *how*. (It is perhaps a little doubtful
if **eu** in Lat. **neuter** is a diphthong. It was certainly
trisyllabic at one period[1].)

(*f*) Lat. **ui** (as in h**ui**c) is very nearly like Fr. *ouï*
(from *ouïr*). But **ui** almost always forms two syllables
as in **mŏnŭī, fŭĭt**. As a diphthong it is a little difficult
to pronounce, the two vowels not coalescing very easily.
The Eng. word *fluid* gives only a rough approximation,
the two vowels fusing only in a very slight degree.

[1] Professor Postgate has pointed out that the pronunciation of **neuter** is
really an unsolved problem. "It is difficult to find a passage in Classical
verse where the first syllable *must be long*. On the other hand, **nĕŭter**
cannot be proved, as there was a form **necuter**, a form which Classical
poets (Lucretius, Seneca, Martial) used if they wanted a trisyllable."

The pronunciation of **cui** and **quī** are often confused. In **quī** the **u** is a consonant, and **qu** = *kw*; thus **quī** = *kwee*, the vowel *i* being clearly pronounced as a simple vowel. In **cui** the **ui** is a diphthong; the word strikes upon the ear as if the spelling were something like '*coo-y*,' but anything of the nature of a disyllable must be avoided.

CHAPTER III

LATIN AND ENGLISH CONSONANTS

17. Consonants are the result of audible friction or stopping of the breath in some part of the mouth or throat.

One convenient basis of classification[1] of consonants depends upon the degree of obstruction of the mouth channel. From this point of view, consonants are either *mutes*, or *continuants*.

If the mouth channel is closed or entirely stopped, an "explosion" takes place when the stoppage is removed. The explosive consonants, also called *mutes*, are six in number; two "labials," *b*, *p*; two "dentals," *d*, *t*; and two so-called "gutturals," *g* (as in *go*), *k*.

If the mouth channel is not quite closed, the obstruction produces a rubbing or "fricative" sound. The fricative consonants are also called *continuants*, since the sound can be kept up by merely continuing the breath. The term continuant is, however, rather loosely used.

---

[1] Consonants are classified on different bases, not always logical in character. Only such points are touched on here as are necessary for dealing with difficulties in Latin.

Certain fricative consonants are known as *liquids*. Two of these, *l* and *r*, call for special notice, as they enter largely into certain Latin consonant combinations. Liquids are formed with so wide a passage, and with so little friction, that they must be regarded as closely akin to the vowels. The consonant *w* is also closely akin to the vowels, as will be seen later on.

Both *l, r* and *w* are sometimes described as " vowel-like " in character.

18. One of the most general principles in speech is to take the shortest way between two sounds in immediate juxtaposition. This often results in combinations without any " glide " at all. Combinations of mutes and the vowel-like consonants *r, l,* and *w* (for instance, *br, pr, dr, tr, gr, kr, bl, pl, cl, gl, kw*) are glideless in both English and Latin, immediate fusion taking place. For all practical purposes, such combinations are simple sounds; there is one and only one effort of the voice made in producing them. This may be tested in such words as *bray, pray, dray, tray, gray, cray* (= *kray*)[1], *play, clay* (= *klay*), *blow, glow, quite* (= *kwite*), &c.

19. It is particularly necessary not to confuse other combinations, especially *sc, sp,* and *st,* with the glideless combinations in the preceding section. Such confusion is the cause of one very common fault in the pronunciation of Latin, as will presently be seen. A distinct effort is experienced in passing from the *s* to the mute. The pronunciation of such pairs of words as *car* and *scar, crawl*

---

[1] Note that in English *c* is a redundant letter, for it has the sound of either *s* or *k*. Other redundant letters are *q*, for *qu* = *kw* ; and *x*, for *x* has either the sound of *ks* as in *extra*, or *gz* as in *exact*.

and *scrawl, pin* and *spin, play* and *splay, top* and *stop, train* and *strain,* should be carefully compared.

The Latin consonants may now be touched upon seriatim.

20. b.—As in English.

21. bs.—Lat. u**rbs**, a**bs**orbeo, as in Eng. cap**s**; never the *bz* sound in Eng. *cabs.* Lat. **s** never takes the Eng. *z* sound, and to preserve the **s** sound in such a word as *urbs,* the **b** naturally passes into *p.* It is a case of the law of least effort[1].

22. bt.—Lat. o**bt**ineo, as in Eng. ke**pt**. In this combination, as in the last, the change from **b** to *p* takes place almost unconsciously. Even in the English word *obtain* some effort is necessary to prevent the *b* from becoming a *p*, and a still greater effort is necessary to preserve the *b* and the *s* in such a word as *absorb*; if the *b* is correctly sounded, the *s* tends to become a *z*; if the *s* is correctly sounded, the *b* tends to become a *p*[2].

It may be noted that *apsens* and *optineo* are good spellings in classical Latin.

23. c.—Lat. **c**ănō, **c**ĕ**c**ĭnī, con**d**ĭ**c**ĭō, as in Eng. **c**ot, **k**ite; never the *s* sound in *circle.* Hence *kekinee, condikio* (never *condishio*).

24. ch.—Lat. pul**ch**er, Ba**cch**us, as Eng. **k** followed by an aspirate; never as in *church* or *chivalry.* The

---

[1] It is possible that in Lat. **bs** the sound began as a *b* and finished as a *p*.

[2] These tendencies are perfectly natural and are easily understood, once the relations amongst the different consonants are understood. Consult any text-book on phonetics.

correct sound can be obtained by pronouncing the words *deck-hand* or *fork-handle* in such a way that the mute *k* comes into the second syllable, e.g., *for-khandle.* The sound is easy to an Irishman. It is better to omit the aspirate altogether, as was done in old and Popular Latin, if there is any difficulty.

25. d.—As in English[1]. But before a word beginning with a consonant, **d** final often becomes a *t*, as in **sed, haud, apud.** So Eng. *tidbit* became *titbit.* Cf. Ger. *unt* for *und.*

26. f.—As in English[2].

27. g.—Lat. **g**audeo, **g**enus, as in Eng. **g**ot, **g**et; never as *j* in *jet* or *g* in *gin.*

28. gn.—After a vowel, as in rēg**num**, cōg**nō**men, **gn** was possibly pronounced **ng-n**, thus **rēng-num, cōng-nōmen.** But on this point there is doubt, and **gn** is best pronounced as in English (e.g. **rēg-num**).

29. gu.—In the combination **gu, u** may be a vowel or a consonant. It is an ordinary vowel in **argŭō**, in perfects in **-gŭī** (e.g. **frĭgŭī**), and in adjectives in **-gŭŭs** (e.g. **ambĭgŭŭs**); in all these cases, **gŭ** has the sound of *goo* in Eng. *good.*

After **n** the **u** in **gu** is generally consonantal.— See § 38.

30. h.—As in English, but more slightly; the breathing must only just be heard. Lat. **h** is sometimes a mere

---

[1] Nearly. In all probability the Latin sound was pronounced with the tongue touching the teeth.

[2] But with more "breath."

sign of hiatus, i.e. it is used to make clear to the eye that the vowels are to be pronounced as two syllables rather than as a diphthong, e.g. in **ahēnus** (another spelling of **aēnus**). Lat. **h** never prevents "slurring" or the shortening of vowels before other vowels (see § 73, &c.), and it often admits contraction, as **nīl** for **nĭhĭl** (or **nĭhīl**).

Lat. **h** never makes position. See § 67.

31. k.—As in English.

32. l.—As in English.

33. m.—As in English, except when final. See § 52.

34. n.—As in English.

35. nc.—Lat. incĭpit. Here **nc = ng + k**; **incipit = ing-kipit.** As in English, *n* before a "guttural" is so affected as to leave its proper sound incomplete (the tongue not touching the roof of the mouth), while it tends to draw the guttural into itself. So Eng. *concord = cong-kord.*

36. nf.—In Latin words, *n* in the combination *nf* had probably lost its consonantal character altogether, leaving the preceding vowel nasalised and long. But it is perhaps best[1] to pronounce the consonantal combination as in English, e.g., Eng. bon-**f**ire. But the preceding vowel in Latin is invariably long; of this there is no doubt whatever. Lat. **cōnficio**, for instance, is pronounced *cone-fikio.*

---

[1] Some classical scholars prefer to omit the *n* altogether, and to nasalise the preceding long vowel. Cf. § 81 (1).

37. ng.—Lat. congero. Here **ng = ng + g**; **congero = cong-gero.** So Eng. *anger = ang-ger* (see § 35 above). Lat. **ng** is never like *ng* in Eng. *singer* or *hanger*.

38. ngu.—In Latin, **u** before another vowel is generally consonantal, and is pronounced as Eng. *w* in *wine*. (See § 55, &c.) Hence from § 37 it follows that **anguĭs** is pronounced **ang-gwis**, and **linguă, ling-gwa**; so with **sanguis, pinguis, unguis, languor,** all of which are, of course, dissyllabic. Cf. Eng. *anguish* (= *ang-gwish*). In such a word as **longŭs**, the **u** is a vowel, and is pronounced in accordance with § 37. Cf. also § 29.

39. nq.—Lat. inquam. Here **nq = ng + q**; **inquam = ing-quam.** So Eng. *relinquish = reling-quish.* Cf. §§ 35 and 37.

40. ns.—In Latin words, *n* in the combination *ns* had probably lost its consonantal character altogether, leaving the preceding vowel nasalised and long (cf. § 36). It is perhaps best[1] to pronounce the consonantal combination as in English, e.g. Eng. **in-s**ight. But the preceding vowel in Latin, as in the case of **nf**, is *invariably long.* Lat. **pīnsō,** for instance, is pronounced *peen-so.*

41. p.—As in English.

42. ph.—Lat. **ph**alerae, **Ph**oebus, as Eng. **p** followed by an aspirate; never as in *Philip* or *elephant*. The correct sound can be obtained by pronouncing the words

---

[1] Some classical scholars prefer to omit the *n* altogether, and to nasalise the preceding long vowel. Cf. §§ 36 and 81 (1).

strap-hanger or *mop-handle* in such a way that the
mute *p* comes into the second syllable, e.g. *stra-
phanger*[1]. If there is any difficulty, it is better to
omit the *h* altogether. Cf. § 24.

43. qu.—Lat. a**qu**ila as in Eng. **qu**een. In Latin, as in
English, **q** is always followed by **u**, and Lat. **qu** = *kw*;
qu must not be regarded as the consonant **q** followed
by the vowel **u**, but as a consonant group *kw*, always
followed by some vowel. The **u** of **qu** must always
be treated as a consonant, just as the second element
of any other consonant group (e.g. **cr**) is treated (see
§ 18); **qu** cannot, of course, form a syllable by itself,
since it is nothing more than a labialised *k*. In verse,
qu is always regarded as a single consonant.

Lat. **qu** is never sounded as in Fr. *quatre*.

44. r.—In sounding **r**, the tongue, after almost touching
the hard palate, is made to vibrate towards the upper
gums. Hence *r* has been called the *trilled* consonant.
Except in the North it is never really heard in
England as a consonant, unless it is followed by a
vowel in the same or in the next word. In the
South of England the words *father* and *farther* are
pronounced exactly alike, though many people experience difficulty in realising this.

Pronounce the words *hear them,* and note that
the *r* is not sounded; there is a mere voice murmur
only.

Now pronounce *hear* in *hear them* exactly as in

---

[1] This suggested pronunciation must not be confused with the pronunciation sometimes given now-a-days to "strap-hanger," viz., "stra-fanger."

hear it. The consonantal sound of the *r* can now be detected.

In Latin, the *r* is always trilled, as in French and Scotch. Lat. rārŭs, dătŏr, as in Fr. dire. The proper rolling of the *r* is extremely important, in finals as well as elsewhere. The English tendency is to slur all unaccented finals. Thus we pronounce **-er, -ir, -ur**, and **-a** without distinction, and as a rule no difference is made between Lat. **mātěr, (a)mātŭr**, and **(a)mātă**. The same vowel sound (and no *r*) is usually given to **vēr, cūr**, and **vĭr** (correctly pronounced weh**r**, koo**r**, and wi**r**). **Arbor** is not *ahba* but ahrbor. The mispronunciation of final syllables ending in *r* is very common even among classical scholars.

Note that such a word as **audīrem** should be pronounced, save for accent, as **audi rem**. An indistinct vowel sound is often wrongly inserted after the **ī** (as in Eng. *dearest*); in other words the pure **i** sound is wrongly converted into a diphthong.

45. rh.—Lat. **rhetor** as in Fr. theatre. (**rh** = Gr. ῥ.) It is the same sound as *r* except that it is *voiceless*, i.e., it is pronounced without the vocal chords vibrating. It is approximately the Eng. initial *r*, as in *rub*, but there is no exact equivalent in English.

46. s.—Lat. **sūs, rŏsă, accūsō**, as in Eng. hiss, hist; never as in Eng. *has* (*haz*). Pronounce **rēs** as *race* (not *reez*), **mōns** as *mohnss* (not *monnz*), **mĭser** as *misser*[1], **rŏsă** as *rossă*[1], **pars** as *parss*. Few letters are so

---

[1] But not, of course, in imitation of a doubled consonant. See Chap. v.

frequently mispronounced as Lat. *s*. Note that
sc = **sk**; pronounce **sciĕntiă** as *skĭĕntiă*, **scītē** as
skītē, &c.

47. su.—In Latin, the **u** in **su** is generally a consonant
(= Eng. *w*) in **suādĕō, suāsī, suāsŭm, suēscō, suēvī,
suētum, suāvĭs, suāvĭtās.** (Pronounce *swahdeo,
swahwis,* &c.) On the rare occasions when the **u** in
suādĕō is a vowel, the word contains four syllables
(**sŭ-ā-dĕ-ō**); so with the other words. The **u** in **su**
is a vowel in **sŭī, sŭŭs, sŭōrum, sŭĕrĕ,** &c. (and of
course in **sūs, sŭpĕr, sūtor,** &c., the **u** being followed
by a consonant : see §§ 59, 61).

48. t.—Always as in Eng. table[1]. Never as in Eng. *nation*
or *edition*. Lat. **ēdĭtiō** is never *edishio*. The sound
of Lat. *t* is invariable.

49. th.—Lat. **thălămŭs, Cĕthēgŭs,** as Eng. *t* followed by an
aspirate, never as in *thin* or *then*. The correct sound
may be obtained by pronouncing the words *gift-horse*
or *hot-house* in such a way that the mute *t* comes
into the second syllable, e.g., *gif-thorse*. If there is
any difficulty the *h* should be dropped altogether.

Note : **ch, ph, th** were introduced in the first
century B.C. to represent, in borrowed words, the
Greek aspirates, which had previously been represented by the simple mutes, e.g., **teātrum,** later
theātrum. They came to be used also in a few
genuine Latin words[2].

All three sounds are easy to Irishmen.

[1] Nearly. Like *d*, the *t* is more "dental" than in English. Fr. table
gives the Lat. **t** more correctly than Eng. table.

[2] But their pronunciation as **c, p, t,** was probably not uncommon.

50. x.—Lat. săxŭm, ĕxŭltō, as in Eng. extra, never the *gz* sound in *example*; **exulto** = *eksulto* (not *egzulto*). Note that **x** is a "double" consonant, and is a mere representative of *cs* or *ks*. **Rĕgsī** (from **rĕgō**) first became **rēcsī**, then **rēxī**.

51. z.—Lat. găză, zōnă, as in Eng. adze, not like *z* in *zeal*. Lat. **z** was certainly a double consonant, for it made "position," and this the Eng. *z* (which is only a voiced *s*)[1] could not do.

---

[1] The distinction between voiced and voiceless consonants is important : Isolate and lengthen the consonant *f* in the word *fit* (-*ffff*-, not the name *ef*), and then the corresponding consonant *v* in the word *liver* (-*vvvv*-, not the name *vee*). Note that while *f* is articulated in one place only, being the result of the friction of the outgoing air between the lower lip and upper teeth, *v* is articulated in two places,—in the throat as well as between lip and teeth.

Place the first two fingers on "Adam's apple." The vibration which produces the effect of voice in *v* can be felt, but this is not so in the case of *f*.

Breathe in the ordinary way, then bring the lower lip and upper teeth together; an *f* is produced. Make a voice murmur, as in *err*, and bring the lip and teeth together ; a *v* is produced.

Do the same with the pair *s* and *z*, first separately and then in one breath,—*ssss*, *zzzz*, *sszz*, *zzss*,—until the distinction is felt and thoroughly under command.

Do the same with the *th* in *thin* and *then*.

Pronounce *kaa* and *gaa*. Now cut off the vowels and try to sound the consonants alone. In the case of the *g* an audible "guggle" is made, but no sound is made in the case of *k*, although there is a feeling of muscular tension in the tongue.

The distinction ought now to be clear. Of the six "mutes," *b*, *d*, and *g* are voiced; *p*, *t*, and *k* are voiceless. Of the continuants, *v*, *w*, *z*, *th*(en), *j*, *y*, and *zh* are voiced ; *f*, *wh*, *s*, *th*(in), *ch*, and *sh* are voiceless. The liquids are voiced.

52. m *final.*—The pronunciation of **m** *final* is not free from doubt, but it was certainly much more weakly sounded than at the beginning or in the middle of a word. In some way or other final *m* was greatly reduced, probably through the lips not being closed to pronounce it. Possibly it was some adumbration of whispered *m.* The facts we are quite sure about are:

(1) Final *m* did not prevent the preceding vowel of its own word, and the initial vowel of the following word, from being reckoned as one syllable, precisely as would have been the case if no *m* had intervened.

(2) Final *m* followed by a word beginning with a consonant invariably made the syllable which it terminated long.

There is some difference of opinion as to the correct method of pronunciation, but the weight of authority is in favour of the following rules:

(1) If the next word begins with a vowel (or *h*), *drop the m,* nasalise the vowel before it, and run on this vowel to the following one. (If this is too difficult, drop the *m* and its preceding vowel altogether.) Thus—

> **fluctum accipit** is pronounced *fluct$^{\breve{u}}$accipit*; alternatively *fluct'accipit.*
>
> **bonam addit** is pronounced *bon$^{\breve{a}}$addit*; alternatively *bon'addit.*

The pronunciation need occasion little difficulty in practice. The **m** must be dropped in any case, and if we simply touch lightly on the vowel remaining (which is always short), and pass on rapidly to the initial vowel of the following word, sufficient nasalisation will be produced almost unconsciously. It is not at all necessary to make a marked effort to nasalise the sound. Neither should the two vowels form a diphthong. The first should only *just* be heard; the second should be distinctly pronounced. Thus the above pairs of words may be written *fluctᵛaccipit* and *bonᵃaddit*.

(2) If the next word begins with a consonant, Ellis was of opinion that while, as before, the *m* should be dropped, its effect should be preserved by pronouncing the initial consonant of the next word as if it were doubled, keeping the vowel before the *m* short, but running it on to the doubled consonant. Thus—

īnfándum rēgína	is pronounced		īnfándurrēgína
jam nox	„	„	jánnóx (not jánnox)
tántum fáta	„	„	tántuffáta
quum pédēs	„	„	quúppédēs
spárgam flórēs	„	„	spárgafflórēs

In all cases the accent remains as if the words were separately pronounced.

But at the present time the weight of opinion is against Ellis, as he is not supported by the facts of the language. The best authorities are strongly in favour of a more "organic" assimilation to the following consonant. Hence the following subsidiary rules:

(α) Before *n, t, d, s,* and perhaps *f, j* (*i* con-

sonant), and *v* (*u* consonant), **m** changes to **n.**
Hence:

jam nox	is pronounced	jánnóx	
ménsam ténet	„	„	ménsanténet
équum dīvínā	„	„	équundīvínā
tántum spērábam	„	„	tántunspērábam
spárgam flórēs	„	„	spárganflórēs
claúim jácit	„	„	claúinjácit
músam vídit	„	„	músanvídit

(*β*) Before *c* (or *q*) and *g*, **m** changes to **ng.**
Hence:

ménsam graúem	is pronounced	ménsanggraúem	
cántum cōnsúltor	„	„	cántungcōnsúltor
uterúm-que	„	„	uterúng-que
quámquam	„	„	quángquam

(*γ*) Before *m*, *b* and *p*, **m** remains **m.** Hence:

mágnam māvórtis	is pronounced	mágnammāvórtis	
quídem bónitās	„	„	quídembónitās
quórum pars	„	„	quórumpárs

(*δ*) Before *l* and *r*, **m** is completely assimilated.
Hence:

jam lābéntibus	is pronounced	jállābéntibus	
īnfándum rēgína	„	„	īnfándurrēgína

Ellis favours dropping the *m* altogether before *j* (consonantal *i*) and *v* (consonantal *u*), and pronouncing the vowel (preceding the *m*) long. Thus:

claúim jácit	would be pronounced	claúījácit	
músam vídit	„	„	„	músāvídit

This may be regarded as an acceptable alternative to (a) above.

(3) It has been suggested that, if the last word of a Latin sentence ends in *m*, the *m* should be sounded very lightly, as in the current pronunciation of Cheltenham, Birmingham (Chelten'm, Birming'm), &c. But this is certainly wrong, for it is always the *m* that is weak, not the vowel. The *m* should be totally inaudible, but the preceding vowel is best sounded long, if only to indicate the excision of *m*.

53. The following English consonantal sounds do not occur in Latin: **ch** in *church*; **j** in *judge*; **sh** in *shall, sure, patient*; **th** in *thin*; **th** in *then*; **wh** (breathed *w*) in *where* (in Scotland); **yh** (breathed *y*)[1] in *human*; **zh** in *pleasure*; **z** in *zealous, rose*.

CHAPTER IV

ɪ AND ᴜ AS CONSONANTS

54. In sounding English **j**, the front of the tongue touches the hard palate; in sounding **y** it comes *near* the hard palate but does not quite touch it. The close relationship between Eng. **j** and Ger. **j** (which is approximately equivalent to Eng. **y**) is thus easily understood.

---

[1] The first element of the diphthong *u* is alone considered in this example. That element does not appear in Lat. long *u*. In Latin, *hu* would be pronounced *hoo*.

In sounding **y** the tongue is very much in the same position as in sounding ɪ (**ee**). This explains why ɪ tends to become **y** before a vowel (e.g., *onion* is pronounced *onyon*). In such words as *yet, yonder*, **y** is virtually a consonant; if however in these words *i* be substituted for *y*, and the words (*iet, ionder*) be rapidly pronounced, the results are practically, if not identically, the same as before.

(The difference between ɪ (= **ee**) and **y** is that in *y* the tongue is put in the *i* position and immediately withdrawn. This makes practically an *action* and so a *consonant*, as opposed to a *position*, i.e., a *vowel*.)

55. The letter **v** is merely another form of **u** and was used either as a vowel or as a consonant. The letter **w** is really a double **v**, though it is called a double **u**.

In such words as *win* and *twice*, **w** is virtually a consonant; if however in these words **u** (= *oo*, as in *food*) be substituted for **w**, and the words (*uin, tuice*) be rapidly pronounced, the results are practically the same as before.

56. Thus both ɪ and **u** when pronounced rapidly before other vowels become virtually consonants, with a distinctive sound of their own. The Romans, though aware of this distinction in sound, made no distinction in writing. But in modern times printers have adopted the practice of using **j** (i.e. *i* with a distinctive tail) for the consonantal sound of ɪ (i.e. for the sound **y**); and of using **v** (a mere variant of **u**) for the consonantal sound of **u** (i.e. for the sound represented by Eng. **w**).

The use of these letters **j** and **v** cannot be justified, and as regards pronunciation is very misleading.

57. Lat. ĭ is consonantal—

(1) When initial and followed by a vowel.

(2) When it occurs between vowels.

Though often printed *j*, it is pronounced as Eng. **y** or Ger. **j**.

Thus ĭăcĭō (jăcĭō) is pronounced yăkĭō

      mālŏr (mājŏr) „   „   mā-yor

      ĭūs (jūs)   „   „   yūss

      āĭō   „   „   ā-yō

      āĭēbam   „   „   ā-yē-bam.

58. In certain words borrowed from the Greek, initial *i* before a vowel is a true vowel, e.g., in **ĭambus.** In other borrowed Greek words, **ĭ** is a true vowel even when between two other vowels, as in **Āglă-ĭ-ă, Lā-ĭ-ŭs.** So in **Gā-ĭ-ŭs.**

But usually in the combinations **ai** and **ei** when followed by a vowel, the **ĭ** both makes a diphthong with the preceding **a** or **e** and is consonantal to the vowel following.

Thus   Staiēnŭs = Stai-yē-nŭs

          Pompēiŭs = Pom-pei-yŭs

          Māiŭs = Mai-yŭs.

59. Consonantal **u** is never found before a consonant and is never used as a final; it occurs invariably before a vowel. Though often printed **v** it is pronounced as Eng. **w** in **wine,** or perhaps still more nearly like Fr. **ou** in *oui* or *ouest*.

Thus

      uĕtō (vĕtō)   is pronounced wĕ-tō

      cīuis (cīvis)   „   „   kee-wiss

      ămāuĭt (ămāvĭt) „   „   ă-ma-wit.

60. It should be clearly understood that the letters **j** and **v** are mere arbitrary signs used by the printer. The Classical Association recommends that the use of **j** shall be entirely discontinued, and that **v** shall be used in books for beginners only.

61. Occasionally consonantal **i** and consonantal **u** may be preceded by a consonant in the same syllable. In, for instance, the word **suāuĭs** (suāvĭs) the consonantal **u** is preceded by **s**; the word is a dissyllable, and is pronounced *swā-wĭs*. (See also § 47[1].)

Note: In this book consonantal *i* and *u* are generally printed *j* and *v* respectively, though in the exercises at the end of the book they are shown by difference of type within the same word, e.g. **i**acio or i**acio** (jacio); ci**u**is or *ciuis* (civis). The symbols *j* and *v* have been retained with considerable reluctance, for there is no justification for their use. But no doubt words containing them will be more familiar to the eye of the ordinary reader, and for this reason they have been preserved. It is however to be hoped that both symbols will soon disappear from all Latin texts.

CHAPTER V

DOUBLED CONSONANTS

62. The correct pronunciation of doubled consonants is of great importance, and for the proper rendering of metre and rhythm, of fundamental importance.

---

[1] Madvig spells *svadeo, qvis*, etc., in his Latin Grammar.

To pronounce a doubled consonant correctly, hold the first element until ready to pronounce the second. The duplication should be regarded as the " energetic utterance " of a single consonant. There should be "no discontinuity of expiration," "no relaxation of the organs"; and "no puff of wind or grunt of voice" should intervene between the two parts of a doubled consonant, which should more resemble separate parts of one articulation than two separate articulations.

Double explosives present some difficulty; double fricatives are more easily managed.

Lat. pe**cc**o,	pronounce as in Eng.		boo**k-c**ase	(not as in *peccant*)
„ pu**pp**is,	„	„	„	ho**p-p**ole	(„ „ *puppet*)
„ gu**tt**a,	„	„	„	coa**t-t**ail	(„ „ *gutter*)
„ ca**nn**ae,	„	„	„	swa**n-n**eck („ „ *cannel*)
„ fo**ss**a,	„	„	„	gra**ss-s**own („ „ *fossil*)
„ mo**ll**is,	„	„	„	ha**ll-l**ight („ „ *Molly*).

Some English speakers, especially on the stage, make a definite break in the articulation of such examples as some of the above, especially in the case of such "explosives" as **t**. But this must be avoided in the case of doubled consonants in Latin.

63. If doubled consonants are correctly pronounced, there can be no confusion between such words as **terras** and **teras**, **mannus** and **manus**. In such words as **teras** and **manus**, particular care should be taken not to double the consonant. The first syllable should be clearly **te-** and **ma-**; the **r** and the **m** respectively belong exclusively to the second syllables. There must be no "glide" of any kind from the **e** to the **r**, or from the **a** to the **n**. (See § 13.)

CHAPTER VI

LATIN SYLLABLES

64. A syllable has been defined as "such a sound or succession of sounds as can be uttered with a single breath impulse." But this definition is not quite accurate, since it does not cover the case of certain *initial* syllables. In the words **scēnă, spătĭŭm, stătĭm, scrībō, splēn, sprētus, strŭō**, the initial consonant combinations **sc, sp, st, scr, spl, spr, str** cannot be uttered with a single breath impulse; in each case the articulation of the mute (**c, p** or **t**) is preceded by a distinct breath effort made for the sibilant **s**. The definition also fails, though in the same slight degree, in the case of certain consonant combinations at the *end* of a syllable, e.g. **urbs**; this, however, is of little importance.

A perfectly satisfactory positive definition of a syllable is difficult to formulate, but the exact significance of the term will be seen from what has already been stated and from what follows.

65. The number of syllables in a word.

(1) Any word in Latin consists of as many syllables as it contains "vowels separately pronounced." Thus **sī, rĕgō, cŏrōnă, băsĭlĭcă, dēlībĕrārĕ, lībĕrālĭtātĕ** contain 1, 2, 3, 4, 5, and 6 syllables, respectively.

(2) For this purpose diphthongs count as single vowels. Thus **caupōnae** contains three syllables. (As all diphthongs are long, it is never necessary to "mark" them.)

(3) When *i* and *u* are used as consonants, they cannot, of course, either alone or with other consonants, form a syllable. Thus **ĭŏcōsē** (= **jŏcōsē**), and **uānĭtās** (= **vānĭtās**) are words of three syllables; **māĭŏr** (**mājŏr**) and **uŏlō** (**vŏlō**), of two syllables. So in such words as **suādĕō** (three syllables), **lĭnguă** (two syllables), **quī** (one syllable), where **u** is a consonant. (Note that **i** and **u** as consonants are not marked. On the rare occasions when the **u** in such a word as **suādĕō** is a vowel, it is, of course, marked; thus **sŭādĕō** contains four syllables.)

66. The division of words into syllables.

(1) A single consonant goes with the following vowel: **dē-lī-bĕ-rā-rĕ, ă-că-dē-mĭ-ă.** If a word ends in a consonant, this final consonant is attached to the last vowel: **cĭ-tĕ-rĭ-ŏr.**

(2) Two consonants coming together are divided: **păl-lĭ-dŭs, mă-gĭs-tĕr, hŏr-tā-băn-tŭr, dĭs-cŭs-sĭ-ō-nĕ.**

(3) The last rule holds good, so far as *sound* (in speech and verse) is concerned, in the "double" consonants **x** and **z**: **exulto** = *ek-sul-to*; **gaza** = *gadza*.

(4) But if the two consonants coming together form a glideless sound-combination (a mute or **f** followed by **r, l,** or consonantal **u,** see § 18), both go with the following vowel, the underlying principle being that such a combination cannot be divided. The fifteen possible combinations may be classified thus:—

1—3; **pr, tr, cr**; *e.g.,* ă-prī-cŭs, pă-trĭs, vŏ-lŭ-crĭs;

4—6; **br, dr, gr**; *e.g.,* lă-tĕ-bră, quă-drŭ-pēs, ă-grĭ-cŏ-lă;

7—8; **pl, cl** ;   *e.g.*, mă-nĭ-plŭs, sē-clū-sŭs ;
9—10; **bl, gl** ;   *e.g.*, pŭ-blĭ-cŭs, rĕ-glū-tĭ-nō ;
11—12; **fr, fl** ;   *e.g.*, vă-fră, rĕ-flŭ-ŭs ;
13—15; **gu, qu, su** ; *e.g.*, lĭn-guă[1], rĕ-quĭ-ēs-cō[2], dē-suē-tŭs[3].

(5) In poetry, many of these consonant combinations are frequently divided, the object being to lengthen the preceding syllable; e.g., **păt-rĭs, vŏ-lŭc-rĭs, lă-tĕb-ră, ăg-rĭ-cŏ-lă.** This is a very important point, as will presently be seen.

(6) If the combinations are themselves preceded by a consonant, the combination still begins the syllable, the other consonant going to the preceding syllable: **mă-gĭs-trō, Dĕ-cĕm-brĭs, cŭl-trī, ĭn-quăm, lĭn-guă.**

(7) Rule (1) holds good for compounds: **ă-dĭ-gō, ŏ-bae-rā-tŭs,** though for the convenience of showing clearly their origin, the compounds are often *written* etymologically (**ăd-ĭgō, ŏb-aerātŭs**).

(8) If, however, the first twelve consonant combinations in Rule (4) are brought about by composition, the mute and the liquid must be kept separate, being pronounced in separate syllables: **ŏb-lā-tŭs** (not **ŏ-blā-tŭs**); **sŭb-lā-tŭs** (not **su-blā-tus**); **ăb-rĭ-pĭ-ō** (not **ă-brĭ-pĭ-ō**); **ăb-rŭm-pō** (not **ă-brŭm-pō**). In such cases there was very little fusion between the mute and the liquid. The prefixes formed distinct words for a very long time.

(9) The consonant combinations in § 64 must not be confused with those in Rule (4) of this section. The

---

[1] See §§ 37, 38.   [2] See § 43.   [3] See § 47.

former, unless initial, are invariably divided[1]; the latter are never divided, except in poetry.   (See Rule (5).)

(10)   The general rule in the case of more than two consonants coming together is that the division falls before the last consonant; or, if the last two consonants form one of the combinations in Rule (4), before that combination: **plānc-tŭs, cōns-cīs-cō, pĕrs-pī-rā-rĕ, pă-lūs-trĭs, īns-trŭ-ō**[2].

---

[1] This is in accordance with the weight of authority, despite Priscian's rules.

[2] From the fifth century of our era onwards, the Roman grammarians laid down the rule that all the consonant combinations which can begin a word must be joined to the succeeding, and not to the preceding syllable (e.g. **a-spice, a-mnis, ca-stra**). But the rule can hardly be correct. It seems probable that certain main principles of phonetics were imperfectly understood.

A final short vowel is rarely lengthened before two consonants at the beginning of the next word.   Instances are occasionally found before *sp, sc, sq, st, gn,* but they are rare; and instances are still more rare before *pr, br, tr,* &c.

The question of syllable division in Latin is by no means free from difficulty.   An interesting paper on the subject appears in *Classical Philology,* Vol. I, No. 1, January, 1906.   It is by Mr Walter Dennison and is entitled " Syllabification in Latin Inscriptions."   The evidence given by the large number of Inscriptions examined, as regards (1) the division of words between lines; and (2) the separation of syllables by interpunctuation (dots), goes to show that the consonantal groups were divided so that the second syllable always began with a group that could begin a *Latin* word. For (1) the percentage was about 80; for (2) much larger.   Thus we have **c-t, g-n, p-t, mp-s,** &c.

There are two apparent anomalies :—

(i)   **m-n** and **-mn** are both found, though **m-n** is more frequent;

(ii)   groups beginning with **s** are divided after the **s**: **s-p, s-t, s-c,** though these groups may begin words in Latin.

Also **ns-t** and **ns-tr** (one instance) are divided as here shown.

(11) A syllable may begin with any vowel, diphthong, single consonant, or any one of the consonant combinations in Rule (4). *Initial* syllables may begin with all these, and, in addition, with those in § 64; also with *gn*, but only in the older language.

(12) The final syllable of a word may end in a short or long vowel, a diphthong, or one or more consonants: **mēn-să, mēn-sā, mēn-sae, rĕ-gĭt, rĕ-gĕnt.**

(13) An aspirated mute though spelled with two letters must be regarded as a single consonant: **ĕ-lĕ-phăs.** In fact, the aspirate may generally be ignored for all purposes of syllabification: **pŭl-chĕr, pŭl-chrē, pă-rŏ-chŭs.**

Length of syllables.

67. The correct pronunciation of Latin depends very largely upon an accurate knowledge of syllable length. *The length of the syllable and the length of the contained vowel are two totally different things,* and must not be confused.

There is an old rule to the effect that a vowel short by nature may become long by position[1] before two consonants.

In face of this evidence we cannot say that a syllable division like **in-strŭō** is wrong.

It is probable that the syllable division in groups containing **s** was not perfectly fixed. Also the fact that in verse some poets lengthen a final syllable that ends in a vowel, and some keep it short, shows that the **s** had a certain mobility, and it was this uncertainty which led most verse-writers to avoid the collocation of short final vowel +**sc, sp,** &c., altogether.

[1] The terms *positione* or *positu* meant originally "by convention."

But a vowel cannot become long by position. If it is naturally short, it remains short; *neither the length nor the pronunciation of the vowel changes.* In the word **nĕctō** the **e** is short; the mere fact that it comes before two consonants does not lengthen it. On the other hand the *syllable* **nĕc-** is long.

Some of the older grammars were in the habit of marking the vowels in such syllables long, e.g., **nēctō**, but this was a serious blunder[1].

A vowel *may* be long before two consonants, e.g., **ē** in **mēnsă**, but that is because it is naturally long. Its "position" has nothing whatever to do with its length. The syllable **men-** would be long whether the vowel **e** was long or not; in the word **mendum**, for instance, the syllable **mĕn-** is long, though the vowel is short.

68. As Ellis pointed out, the most artificial part of Latin quantitative rhythm consisted in taking the short vowel or short syllable as the unit of length and supposing that it was always of the same length, and that the long vowel or syllable was exactly twice that length. Nothing of the kind is likely to have occurred in speech or declamation. Still, to begin with, this artificiality must certainly be aimed at, because we have nothing like it in English except in barred music. This is necessary if only in order to destroy our modern Western habits, in which quantitative rhythm is not known.

---

[1] Even Kennedy did this (*Grammar*, pp. 6, 513). No doubt there are reasons of typography that make it difficult to mark the length of the syllables otherwise than by putting a long mark over the vowel. In graduses it is the established practice and in these it ought not to mislead. But the practice is open to objection, for it certainly does mislead,—even students of older growth.

69. Every long vowel must then, in practice, be regarded as equivalent to *two* "times" (pendulum beats, for instance), and a short vowel to *one*. Musically, a long vowel may be compared to a crotchet and a short vowel to a quaver. A consonant, when considered, must be regarded as equal to a short vowel[1].

Syllables are long or short according as they require "two times" or "one time" to pronounce. But in estimating the length of a syllable, the length of time occupied by the consonants *preceding* the vowel is disregarded, even when there are two or three, as in **sta-, scri-.** *The vowel alone counts, or if the vowel be* followed *by a consonant, the vowel and that consonant.*

70. In the following words, a figure *2* is placed under a long syllable, and a figure *1* under a short syllable:

ă-nĭ-mă   rō-bŏ-rō   lē-gā-tī   splĕn·dĭ-dē
1 1   2 1 2   2 2 2   2 1 2

dē-suē-tū-dō   ăs-pĕc·tō   dē-flă-grō   dĭs-cĭ-plī-nă
2 2 2 2   2 2 2   2 1 2   2 1 2

The length of the final syllables of a word should be considered in connection with the initial syllable of the following word:

hŏmĭnĭs ănĭmă   = hŏ-mĭ-nĭ-să-nĭ-mă
                   1 1 1 1 1

hŏmĭnĭs cŏrpŭs   = hŏ-mĭ-nĭs-cŏr-pŭs
                   1 1 2 2

jūdĭcăt ĕnĭm sēnsŭs = jū-dĭ-că-tĕ-nĭm-sēn-sŭs
                       2 1 1 1 2   2

---

[1] This rule is sufficiently exact for its purpose, though it ignores refinements. Of course the length of a consonant differs in different positions, e.g., in bub*bl*ing and bu*lb*ous, *cl*ear and ta*lc*. But see the next paragraph

bŏnă stătĕră[1]   = bŏ-năs-tă-tē-ră (cf. § 64)
                         1   2   1   2

bŏnă crētă   = bŏ-nă-crē-tă (cf. § 66, Rule 4)
                         1   1   2

bŏnō pŭĕrō   = bŏ-nō-pŭ-ĕ-rō
                         1   2   1 1 2

The *final* syllable of a final word in a clause may be considered short if it ends in a short vowel, or a short vowel and consonant[2]. If it contains a long vowel, it is, of course, long in any case. (With reference to "elision" of vowels, see the next chapter.)

71. Briefly:

    (*a*) A syllable is *short* when it ends in a short vowel.

    (*b*) A syllable is *naturally long* when it contains a long vowel.

    (*c*) A syllable is *long by position* when it ends in a consonant. But as a syllable cannot end in a consonant unless the next syllable begins with a consonant, we have the practical rule that *a syllable containing a vowel immediately followed by two consonants is long by position* (the glideless combinations in § 66, Rule 4, of course excepted[3]).

---

[1] This is a very rare type of sequence (i.e. a short vowel followed by initial *st* or any other combination of § 64). Cf. the second and last paragraphs of footnote 2, pp. 34, 35.

[2] But the length of a final syllable having a short vowel was unsettled, and a short syllable might be used as a long one. At the end of a sentence, a syllable was no doubt often lengthened. Whenever there is a pause of necessity, a short syllable with that pause may count as a long one. So at the end of a verse.

[3] But these combinations often make "position" in poetry. (See § 66, Rule 5.)

The explanation of the lengthening "by position" lies in the phonetic division of the syllables. A consonantal combination shared between two syllables lengthens the preceding syllable; a consonantal combination not shared between them leaves the preceding syllable short. Strictly, it is not the consonants which add length, but the pause which separates them.

In the following line—

Dividi**mus m**uros et moenia pandi**mus u**rbis

note that the first **-mus** is a long syllable, and the second **-mu(s)** short. So with the syllable **-ter** in the following line—

Tractus u**ter p**lures lepores, u**ter e**ducet apros.

72. The artificial nature of the rule laid down in § 69, i.e. of taking the short vowel as the unit of length, of regarding the long vowel as equal to two of these units, and a following consonant as equal to one, is seen in such a word as **pŏtēns**, in which the relative length of the syllables might be 1 : 4 (pŏ-tēns). This would be absurd.

In practice, all syllables, however constituted, must be regarded as having one of two time values. They must be either *short* or *long*, and the short syllable is always approximately half the length of the long syllable. As regards time, a succession of syllables is closely analogous to a succession of crotchets and quavers, the crotchets and quavers always accurately preserving their relative length[1]. **Lē-gā-tī** or **trī-gĭn-tā** takes twice as long to pronounce as

---

[1] It may be stated that there is evidence of variable or intermediate length of syllables. But any attempt to imitate them is bound to end in failure.

rĕ-gĕ-rĕ or **lă-crĭ-mă.**   One of the commonest faults is to make the accented syllable of a word long, and all the other syllables short, without regard to their real length.   The question of accent will be considered in Chap. 9.

Note.—A long syllable which is "long by position" is scanned long in Latin poetry, for, even though it have a short vowel, the consonant group following requires a certain period of time for pronunciation[1].   If such a syllable contained a naturally long vowel there would be really extra length, but there is no account taken in Roman poetry of the different length, of, say, the second syllables of **calēsco** and **modĕstus**, both being treated as long syllables.—Cf. Lindsay, § 142, with §§ 67—69 *supra.*

CHAPTER VII

ELISION OF VOWELS.   SLURRING

73.   In the English lines,

"Await alike the inevitable hour,"

and "Hurled headlong flaming from the ethereal sky," the vowel sound of the word *the* does not entirely disappear. It is touched upon very lightly.

So in Latin.   The Romans much disliked the clashing of a final vowel with the initial vowel of the next word.   For correct enunciation, when a final vowel stands before an initial vowel, it should be lightly and shortly pronounced, and run on to the following word.   The final vowel should not be elided entirely, though this is much preferable to

[1] Cf. the first paragraph on p. 39.

having hiatus, a practice which, as Professor Postgate points out, Cicero protested against in the most explicit language. Thus

ego eo	is pronounced	*eg°eo* (not *eg'eo*)
ille ibit	„ „	*ill^eibit* (not *ill'ibit*)
quaeque ipse	„ „	*quaequ^eipse* (not *quaequ'ipse*)
Roma urbs	„ „	*Rom^aurbs* (not *Rom'urbs*)

Although in these cases the final vowel is just heard, it does not, of course, form a syllable. *Rom^aurbs* = two syllables, not three. (Cf. § 52.)

74. The slurring takes place even if the letter *h* begins the second word: *bona haec = bon^ahaec; anima horret = anim^ahorret.*

When the two vowels are the same, the first is suppressed almost entirely: practically, *ergo omnis = ergomnis = er-gom-nis; Marcella amat = Marcellamat = Mar-cel-la-mat.* The effect is very much like that of a single word.

So when a final vowel is followed by a diphthong beginning with the same vowel: *contra audentior = contraudentior = con-trau-den-ti-or.*

75. In such a line as the following

Vēnĕrăt īnsānō Căssăndrae ĭncēnsŭs ămōrĕ

(Vē-nĕ-ră|tīn-sā|nō Căs|săn-dr^aĭn|cēn-sŭ-să|mō-rĕ)

the slurring of the **ae** in **Cassandrae** naturally causes the **e**, almost or entirely, to disappear, and there is a *tendency* for the **a** to fuse with the **i** and form a diphthong. Thus, although it is the first vowel which must always be elided, the vowel if long or if a diphthong, may tend to overwhelm (so to speak) a following short vowel, especially if this vowel is in an unaccented syllable. In the above case the vowel **i** must be distinctly pronounced with its own (short) quantity, the **a** of the **ae** in **Cassandrae** being only just heard. (The ĭ, though short, happens to occur in a syllable long by position.)

But in verse a final long vowel is not often followed by an initial short vowel. This is what might be expected, as a long vowel is, naturally, much less easily sacrificed than a short vowel. Even in the case of short vowels, some are more easily elided[1] than others; for instance, ĕ and ĭ elide more freely than ă and ŏ before a short vowel.

Much as hiatus was disliked it was permitted at the end of one verse before an initial vowel in the next verse; and it is found occasionally even in the same verse, e.g.,

Pŏsthăbĭ|tā cŏlŭ|ĭssĕ Să|mō. Hīc | Illĭŭs | ărmă.

Here the long **o** of **Samō** is preserved.

76. But in prose the general rule must always be followed, viz., the final vowel, whether long or short, of the first word must be only lightly pronounced and run into the initial vowel of the following word. This must be done in such a way that the two syllables are reduced to one. No extra time must be taken, even when a long vowel or a diphthong is elided. Only the *quality* of the elided vowel must be heard. The resulting *quantity* must be entirely that of the initial vowel of the following word.

The same rule should be observed in verse. Exceptions are numerous, but these are always pointed out by good commentators.

---

[1] The word "elision" must not be taken in its literal sense of absolute suppression. "Slurring" is perhaps the better term. The "elided" vowel *very nearly* disappears, but not quite.

77. Within words, open concurrence (hiatus) of vowels is very common, but even here it is avoided in different ways:

(1) The former vowel may be cut off: **ne-ullus =
   nullus.**

(2) The **m** often disappears with its vowel: **animum-
   adverto = animadverto.**

(3) Two concurring vowels unite into one long vowel:
   prŏ-ŏles = prōles; prŏ-ĕmo = prōmo.

In poetry, two vowels were sometimes uttered as forming one syllable, as **aurēā, omnīā**, no written contractions being indicated.

CHAPTER VIII

QUANTITY

78. Accurate pronunciation of Latin is out of the question unless the natural length of every vowel is known. The difference between long and short vowels was undoubtedly very marked in classical Latin, certainly as much as between such English words as *rod* and *rode* or *shin* and *machine.* It has already been stated that there is evidence of some syllables being of intermediate length, and it is quite possible that when a long vowel was followed by two or more consonants the syllable was longer than a long vowel alone. But on these points the evidence which we can regard as unquestioned is very scanty, and it is admitted by competent scholars that the only practical course is to consider the short syllable as the equivalent in length of a short vowel, and the long syllable that of the long vowel, the latter being twice the length of the former. It is, however, a fact, that very few syllables in Latin consist of *a long vowel*, or of *a short vowel, only*. Most have a consonant preceding the vowel, e.g., *nō-tă*.

Long vowels are indicated thus: **ā**, **ē**, &c.; and short vowels thus: **ă**, **ĕ**, &c. Many books leave short vowels unmarked, or, at most, only mark those likely to be thought long.

Beginners in Latin would do well to mark the long vowels of every new word. Such a rule would save them much trouble later on, and would go far to ensure an accurate pronunciation. It is to be regretted that the writers of many grammars are so careless in this matter of marking the vowels, and few even of the best dictionaries consistently mark the vowels in final syllables.

79. The principles underlying composition, substitution, contraction, and other changes, all influencing vowel length, form too vast a subject to be dealt with in detail here. But numerous facts may be grouped together in such a way as to make it possible to formulate useful rules as aids to memory. The following rules deal with the length of vowels in

I. Final syllables: (*a*) ending in a vowel; (*b*) ending in a consonant.

II. Syllables not final.

Monosyllables are included under " final " syllables. (As will be seen, *the vowels in most monosyllables are long*, but there are numerous exceptions.)

I (a). Final syllables ending in a vowel.

A final is short: *mēnsă, audācĭă, mălă, ĭtă, quĭă*, &c., &c.

Except (1) Abl. sing. of A nouns : *mēnsā, pŏētā*, &c.

(2) Imper. sing. act. of A verbs: *ămā, dā*, &c.

(3) Most indeclinable words in *a*: *ergā, quadrā-gintā*, &c.

E final is short: *lēgĕ* (from *lēx*), *lĕgĕ* (from *lĕgō*), *tĭmētĕ, ămārĕ, -quĕ, -nĕ.*

Except (1) Abl. sing. of E nouns : *făcĭē, dĭē*[1].

(2) Imper. sing. act. of E verbs: *mŏnē, tĕnē*, &c.

(3) Adverbs from adjs. of 1st and 2nd declens. : *rēctē, altē, dŏctē*[2], &c.

(4) Monosyllables (enclitics excepted): *ē, dē, mē, sē, tē, nē.*

I final is long: *plēbī, dŏlī, illī, cōnsŭlī, dī, mī, sī*, &c.

Except[3] (1) *nĭsĭ, quăsĭ.*

---

[1] So *hŏdĭē* but *hĕrĕ* (a weakened form of *hĕrī*).

[2] So *fĕrē, fĕrmē, pĕrĕgrē, ohē, valdē, vērē*, but *bĕnĕ, mălĕ, infĕrnĕ, supĕrnĕ.*

[3] The short *i* and *o* forms in many of the exceptions given, and likewise the short *e* in *bĕnĕ* and *mălĕ*, represented originally long vowels or diphthongs, e.g. *mŏdŏ* from *mŏdō, bĕnĕ* from *bĕnē.* The change was due to a process known as iambic shortening. In words of two syllables the first of which was short, there was a marked tendency to shorten the final syllable if long, that is to change the word rhythm from ˇ – to ˇ ˇ. This was not a mere matter of poetic usage but a characteristic of common speech. In isolated forms, such as those mentioned the tendency had full sway, and the short vowel is prevalent from the earliest period. In *mihi*, &c., the form with the short vowel became established but the poets continued to use also the old form *mihī*, &c., at all periods.

As Professor Postgate points out, the shortening of *-ō* began in iambic verbs, spread to cretics, as *dēsĭnō* (*-ŏ* in Tibullus), and these, possibly by analogy, to verbs of different scansions.

(2) *mĭhĭ, tĭbĭ, sĭbĭ, ŭbĭ*[1], *ĭbĭ* (commoner than *mĭhī*, &c.).

O final is long : *multō, jŭvō, ămō, bŏnō, carbō, ŏrīgō, dō, nō,* &c.

Except[2] (1) *ĕgŏ, cĭtŏ, dŭŏ, cĕdŏ, mŏdŏ, quōmŏdŏ.*

    (2) Sometimes *scĭŏ, nescĭŏ, pŭtŏ, vŏlŏ,* and other verbs when used parenthetically, and often in poetry.

    (3) Sometimes *nēmŏ, hŏmŏ.*

    (4) *Scīpĭō, Nāsŏ,* and other proper nouns often end in *ŏ.*

    (5) In post-Augustan writers, *virgŏ, ergŏ, octŏ, porrŏ, immŏ, sērŏ, intrŏ,* &c.

U final is long : *tū, dictū, dĭū,* &c.

Y final is short: *Tĭphŷ, chĕlŷ.*

Summary : final i, o, and u are long[3] **; final a, e, and y are short.**

I (b). Final syllables ending in a consonant.

(1) The vowel in a final syllable ending in any consonant except *s* is short[4].

Examples:

-b : *ăb, ŏb, sŭb.*

-c : *făc, nĕc, dŏnĕc.* (But *lāc, dīc, sīc, hōc, dūc, hūc.*)[5]

-d : *ăd, ĭd, quĭd, quŏd, illŭd.*

---

[1] Note compounds: *ŭbĭnam, ŭbĭvis,* but *ŭbĭquĕ.*

[2] See note 3 on p. 45.   [3] This will suggest a simple mnemonic.

[4] Exceptions are fairly numerous, though most of the important ones are mentioned, except those in *-x* which are many.

[5] Also *illĭc* and *istĭc.* Note that most of the examples of long vowels before *c* are shortened words, not original monosyllables.

-l: *fĕl, mĕl, vĕl, nĭhĭl* (or *nĭhīl*), *Hannibăl*. (But *sāl, sōl, nīl*.)

-m: *dĭĕm, hastăm, ūnŭm, quĭdăm, ămĕm, mŏnĕăm,* &c., &c.

-n: *ăn, ĭn, agmĕn,* &c., &c. (But *ēn, quīn, sīn, nōn, liēn, sīrēn*.)

-r: *fĕr, pĕr, tĕr, cŏr, calcăr, ămābĭtŭr, rĕgĭtŏr, Hectŏr,* &c. (But *Lār, pār, vēr, cūr, fūr, crātēr, āēr, aethēr*.)

-t: *dăt, ĕt, flĕt, tŏt, ămăt, ămāvĭt,* &c. (But note contracted perfects, *īt, audīt,* &c.)

x: *făx, vĭx, pĭx, mŏx, nŏx, nŭx, dŭx, crŭx, vindĕx, fīlĕx,* &c. (But *pāx, rēx, vōx, lūx, līmāx, rādīx, cervīx,* &c.)[1]

(2) The vowel in a final syllable ending in *s* varies as follows:

-as is long: *ămās, terrās, mŏnĕās, mĭsĕrās, ās, fās, vās* (*vāsis*), &c. (But *anăs, văs* (*vădĭs*), *lampădăs, Iliăs, Crātērăs* (*acc. pl.*).)

-es is long: *sēdēs, mŏnēs, audīrēs, vĭdērēs, ēs* (*ĕdō*), *părĭēs,* &c. (*ēs* is a little uncertain).

Except (*a*) Nouns in *ĕs* (with consonant stems) having genitives in[2]:

    (α) *-ĕtĭs*, e.g., *sĕgĕs, tĕgĕs, interprĕs,* &c.

    (β) *-ĭtĭs*, e.g., *ĕquĕs, pĕdĕs, mīlĕs, cŏmĕs, hospĕs,* &c.

    (γ) *-ĭdĭs*, e.g., *obsĕs, praesĕs*.

    (*b*) *ĕs* (*esse*), *pĕnĕs, Arcadĕs, crātērĕs* (n.pl.).

---

[1] Note that *x* is really a compound sound. The vowel usually follows the quantity of the stem: *pāx=pāc-s*; *rēx=rēc-s* (*rĕg-is*): &c.

[2] Note that *pēs, quadrupēs, ābĭēs, ărĭēs, părĭēs,* and many others come under the rule and not under the exceptions.

-is is short: *ēnsĭs, rēgĭs, cŭcŭmĭs, cŭcŭmĕrĭs, ūtĭlĭs, dĭcĕrĭs,* &c., &c.

> Except (*a*) Dat. and Abl. plu. *mēnsīs, vōbīs, quīs, bŏnīs,* &c., &c. So *grātīs, forīs.*
>
> (*b*) Acc. pl. *omnīs, fīnīs,* &c.
>
> (*c*) Indic. pr. 2 sing. of I verbs, as *audīs;* also *possīs, vĕlīs, nōlīs,* &c.
>
> (*d*) Subj. perf. 2 sing., as *ămāvĕrĭs* (but sometimes *ămāvĕrĭs*)[1].
>
> (*e*) *Samnīs, Quirīs, Eleusīs, Salamīs,* &c.

-os is long: *flōs, ōs (ōris), sacerdōs, ventōs, mōs,* &c., &c.

> Except *compŏs, impŏs, ŏs (ossis), exŏs, Argŏs, Dēlŏs, chlămȳdŏs* (Gk. gen. s.).

-us is short: *ŏpŭs, intŭs, ămāmŭs, ămābāmŭs, gĕnŭs, hostĭbŭs,* &c., &c.

> Except (*a*) Gen. sing. and Nom. Acc. pl. of U nouns, as *exercĭtūs.*
>
> (*b*) Nouns in -*us* which increase in the Gen. with a long penult: *tellūs, pălūs, virtūs, incūs, sĕnectūs, jŭventūs, jūs,* &c.
>
> (*c*) Some Greek nouns: *Sapphūs* (gen. s.), *Panthūs* (n. sing.), &c.

II. Syllables not final. There is far too great a variation in the quantity of vowels in syllables not final for rules with any approach to completeness to be possible, and a thoroughly good dictionary becomes absolutely necessary.

---

[1] The converse is the case with the indic. fut. perf.

A few helpful rules may however be given:

(1) All diphthongs are long[1]: *caudae, foedŭs,* &c.

(2) Vowels which have originated from contraction or represent diphthongs are long: *cō-gō* from *cŏ-ăgo*; *mōmentum* for *mŏvĭ-mentum*; *nīl* for *nĭhĭl*[2]; *existĭmō* for *ex-aestĭmō,* &c.

(3) The quantity of the radical syllable of a word is generally preserved in derivation and composition, even when the vowel is changed: *māter, mātĕrnŭs; scrībo, scrīptor; caedō, incīdō; cădō, ĭncĭdō;* &c. But exceptions are numerous.

(4) A vowel before another vowel is short: *prŭs, vĭă, rătĭō,* &c. The rule holds good even if an *h* intervenes: *contrăhĭt, dĕhīscō.*

Exceptions: (*a*) Genitives of pronouns, &c., in *-ius*: *ĭllīus, alīus, solīus, totīus, unīus,* &c. But the *i* in several of these genitives is sometimes short.

(*b*) Old genitives of the first declension, like *aulāī.*

(*c*) Genitives and datives of the fifth, when a vowel precedes: *dĭēī,* but *fĭdĕī.*

(*d*) The *a* or *e* before *i* in proper nouns in *-ius: Gāiŭs, Pompēiŭs.* (But cf. § 58.)[3] Also *plēbēiŭs.*

---

[1] The diphthong *ae* in *prae* in composition becomes short before a vowel, as in *praeesse, praeire.* Practically the *e* is suppressed, and *prae* is pronounced *pră.*

[2] Or *nĭhil.*   [3] The vocatives **Gāī** and **Pompēī** are of similar scansion.

(e) The *i* in the syllable *fī* of *fīō, fīunt, fīēbam,* &c. But it is short before *-er: fĭĕrem,* &c.

(f) In *dīŭs* (adj.), *āēr, āĕra, Aenēās.*

(g) The vowel *i* is generally long before consonantal *u: dērīuō (dērīvō), pĕtīuī (pĕtīvī),* &c. (But *bĭvĭŭm (bĭvĭŭm), trĭuĭŭm (trĭvĭŭm)*.)

The quantity of a vowel followed by two consonants is a case of special difficulty, and is dealt with in the next chapter.

CHAPTER IX

HIDDEN QUANTITY

80. In the vast majority of English words a vowel followed by two consonants is short. We say, for instance, *lŏst,* not *lōst; cŏncert,* not *cōncert.* This is exactly what we should expect when we remember "the law of least effort." An additional effort is required to effect the pronunciation of the two consonants, and the shortening of the vowel sound is the natural consequence. But there are many exceptions. We do not say, for instance, *tŏld,* but *tōld;* not *bĭnd* but *bīnd.*

So it was in Latin. In the great majority of Latin words, a vowel followed by two consonants is short. Still, there is a large number of exceptions, probably more than we are acquainted with, for our knowledge of them is incomplete. The quantity of many vowels followed by two consonants is therefore said to be "hidden," though the term "hidden" is sometimes applied to the quantity of those long vowels (followed by two consonants) that are *known* to us.

Clearly, then, a vowel before two consonants is sometimes naturally short, sometimes naturally long, although the *syllable* containing such a vowel is, as a rule, long. (Cf. Chap. 6.) It is not correct to pronounce the vowel invariably short, as is commonly done. Whenever the vowel is known to be long, as it is in a large number of cases, it must be pronounced long.

In some words the length of the vowel before two consonants has not been determined. The phonetic law of least effort leads us to think that in most of such cases the vowel was *probably* short. The safe plan, therefore, is to pronounce all such vowels short unless they are known to be long.

81. The quantity of a long vowel followed by two consonants is known with certainty in a large number of instances. In other instances there is a strong probability of the vowel being long. In others, authorities are divided in opinion. In still others, there is merely a slight presumption in favour of a long vowel. The following rules are in accordance with the weight of authority.

(1) Vowels are always long before **ns**, **nf**: *dēns, mēns, frōns, pōns, mōns, mēnsa, ingēns, sapiēns, amāns, monēns, nōlēns, cōnspiciō, cōnstituō, cōnsulō, cōnstō, expānsum, mānsum, pānsum, prānsum, scānsum, cēnsum, dēfēnsum, extēnsum, mēnsum, pēnsum, sēnsum, pīnsō, pīnsitum, spōnsum, tōnsum, tūnsum,* &c., &c.

cōnficiō, cōnfiteor, cōnfīrmō, cōnfundō, cōnfluēns, īnfāns, īnfēlīx, īnfēnsus, īnferior, īnfimus, īnfrā, &c., &c.

It has already been said (§§ 36, 40) that **n** before **s** or **f** was probably a mere nasal, lengthening the preceding vowel. Hence some scholars, in pronouncing these words, prefer to omit the *n* altogether; they would pronounce *cōnsul* either as *cō-sul* or as *cō-sul*[1]. There is no objection to this, provided the vowel is kept long.

(2) When a **g** becomes **c** before **t** or **s** the preceding vowel becomes long: *āctum* (from ăgō), *lēctus* (lĕgō), *rēctum* (rĕgō), *tēctum* (tĕgō), *afflīctum* (afflīgō), *frīctum* (frīgō), *sūctum* (sūgō); so *rēxī = rēcsī* (rĕgō), *tēxī = tēcsī* (tĕgō); also *rēx*, *lēx*, &c.

Likewise *frāctum, pāctum, tāctum* (from frango, pango, tango); but *fīctum, pīctum, strīctum* (fingo, pingo, stringo) are a little doubtful.

Contrast *făctum* (from făciō), *năctus* (nancīscor), *păctus* (pacīscor), *trăctus* (trăhō), *ēnĕctum* (ēnĕcō), *sĕctum* (sĕcō), *īnspĕctum* (īnspĭciō), *vĕctus* (vĕhō), *dĭctum* (dīcō), *vĭctum* (vĭncō)[2], *ĭctus* (īcō), *frĭctum* (frĭco), *cŏctum* (cŏquō), *dŭctum* (dūcō), in which the **c** does not come from a **g**.

Note: It should be noticed that the lengthening of the vowel before **ct** or **cs**, when the **c** comes from a **g** is a change in perfect harmony with the ordinary laws of phonetics.

(3) As might be expected from the preceding rule, the vowel is usually long before **nct** and **nx**: *cīnctum, cīnxī* (cingō); *fīnxī* (fingō); *exstīnctum, exstīnxī* (exstinguō); *strīnxī* (stringō); *tīnctum, tīnxī* (tinguō); *fūnctus* (fungor); *jūnctum, jūnxī* (jungō); *pūnctum* (pungō); *ūnctum, ūnxī* (unguō). There is some slight doubt about *plānctum, plānxī* (plangō); *pīnxī* (pingō); and *dīstīnctum, dīstīnxī* (dīstinguō). On the other hand, there is some authority

---

[1] ŏ is a nasalised *o*.   [2] But *victum* (from vīvo).

for *nānctus* (nancīscor); *sānctum, sānxī* (sanciō); *vīnctum, vīnxī* (vinciō), although in these cases the **c** does not come from a **g**.

When the phonetic laws of the Latin language are better known, it is highly probable that the present slight doubt about *fīctum, pīctum, strīctum, plānctum, plānxī, pīnxī, dīstīnctum, dīstīnxī*, will disappear; also that the long vowel now suggested, by one or two authorities, in *nānctus, sānctum, sānxī, vīnctum, vīnxī* will prove to be short.

(4) A vowel is long before **ps** and **pt** when these come from **bs** and **bt**: *scrīpsī, scrīptus* (from scrībō); *nūpsī, nūptum* (nūbō). In these cases note the long vowel in the present indicative.

(5) The vowel in nominatives ending in **-x, -ps, -bs** is long if long in the other cases: *lēx* (*lēgis*), *Cyclōps* (*Cyclōpis*), *plēbs* (*plēbis*), &c.

(6) There was a general tendency to lengthen a vowel before **r** *followed by another consonant*, and in the case of many words the pronunciation of the vowel as a long vowel became the recognised one. This is true of *Mārs, Mārcus, Mārcius, Lārs, ōrdō, ōrdior, ōrnō, fōrma, quārtus*, and several others.

(7) The vowel is usually long before **gn**; *āgnus, māgnus, māgnitudō, stāgnum, rēgnum, sēgnis, dīgnus, sīgnum, īgnis, līgnum, pūgna, pūgnō, āgnātiō, āgnōmen, āgnōscō, cōgnātus, cōgnitus, cōgnōmen, cōgnōscō, īgnāvia, īgnōbilis, īgnōminia, īgnōscō, īgnōtus, īgnārus, prīvīgnus*, &c.

In some of these cases it has been established beyond doubt that the vowel was long by origin, and it is known that the pronunciation of the vowel as a long vowel existed in other cases. But there is still much doubt about Roman general practice.

(8) A vowel is long before **sc** in verbs in **-sco** : *pāscō, nāscor, crēscō, compēscō, scīscō, nancīscor, ulcīscor, oblīvīscor, profīcīscor, nōscō, āgnōscō, cōgnōscō, īgnōscō,* &c., &c. There is a little doubt about *dīscō, compēscō* and *pōscō,* but they probably follow the general rule.

(9) Shortened perfect forms in **-āsse, -ēsse, -īsse, -āstī, -ēstī, -īstī,** &c., have a long vowel before the **s** : *amāsse, amāssem, dēlēsse, dēlēssem, audīsse, audīssem, amāstī, amāstis, dēlēstī, dēlēstis, audīstī, audīstīs, nōsse, nōstī,* &c.

(10) In a considerable number of words, the long **a** which comes before two consonants is explained by derivation. Thus we have *frātricīda* from *frāter, mātrimōnium* from *māter.* So with the long **o** in such a word as *sōlstitium* from *sōl.*

(11) The long **a** in derivatives in *-ātrum, -ābrum,* &c., is also obviously derived from a principal; thus we have *flābrum* from *flāre*; *dolābra* from *dolāre*; *lābrum, lavābrum,* and *lavācrum,* from *lavāre*; *arātrum* from *arāre*; *simulācrum* from *simulāre*; &c.

(12) The quantity of a long vowel in a principal is *generally* the same in compounds, derivatives, and parallel formations. Thus we know that the **a** in *āctum* is long, and we may therefore infer *āctiō, āctor, adāctum, co-āctum, perāctum,* &c. Similarly *frōndis*[1] (*frōns*) implies *frōndōsus ; vēndō* implies *vēndidī* and *vēnditum ; nūntiō* implies *nūntius.* So with *scrīptus, scrīptor ; ārdeō, ārdēscō ; pūrgō, pūrgātiō ; fōrma, fōrmō, fōrmula ; fīrmus, fīrmō, fīrmāmentum ;*

---

[1] Lewis. (But doubtful.)

ūsūrpō, ūsūrpātiō; nārrō, nārrātus, nārrātor; ōsculum, ōsculor; ōscitō, ōscitāns; prōsperus, prōsperō; prōspiciō, prōspectus; rēctum, dīrēctum, perrēctum, surrēctum; and so on.

(13) In such Greek-borrowed words as *pēgma, Mētrodōrus* and *mētropolis,* the long vowel before the two consonants is simply the reproduction of the Greek long vowel.

82. Long vowels are frequently met with before other pairs of consonants, and it occasionally happens that no principle or rule concerning them is discoverable[1]. The reader is advised to make a list for himself as he comes across them in his reading. No authoritative list of such words, or at all events no exhaustive list, has yet been published. It is difficult, in fact, to prepare such a list, in view of the difference of opinion about certain words. The following list is by no means exhaustive, but it will suffice to give the reader some idea of the variety of forms he may expect to meet with.

(i) Long vowels before glideless combinations of consonants. (Cf. § 66 (4).)

br. *crābrō, candēlābrum, ēbrius, lībra, crībrum, sōbrius, lūbricus, delūbrum.* (See also Rule 11.)

cr. *mūcrō, involūcrum.* (See also Rule 11.)

dr. *dōdrāns.*

gr. *dīgredior* (and therefore *dīgressus,* &c.), *vēgrandis,* and possibly *frāgrāns*[2].

tr. *ātrium, clātrī, lātrō* (bark), *lātrīna, cicātrīx, quīnquātrūs, nūtriō, nūtrīx, vērātrum.* (See also Rules 10 and 13.)

---

[1] On the other hand, the origin of the long vowel is often obvious, e.g. *pūrgō* from *pùrigō, lārdum* from *lāridum, lāmna* from *lāmina, pulvĭllus* dim. of *pulvinus,* and so on.   [2] Lewis. (But very doubtful.)

bl. *pūblicus* (*pūblicō, pūblicē*, &c.).
cl. *perīclitor.*
gl. *dīgladior, iūglāns.*

(ii) Long vowels before certain **s** groups of consonants. (See § 64.)

sc. *ōsculum* (*ōsculor*), *ōscitō* (*ōscitāns*), *vāsculum, ēsca, sēscuncia, sēscentī, prīscus, rōscidus, mūscus,* and probably *lentīscus, vīscus.* (See also Rule 8.)

sp. *prōsperus, prōspiciō, āspernor, sōspita* and *sōspes;* probably *crīspus;* possibly *sūspīciō* (noun) and *sūspĭciō* (verb).

st. *fāstus* (court-day), (*nefāstus*), *pāstum, pāstor, pāstillus, vāstus, nāsturcium, bēstia, comēstum, fēstus, palimpsēstus, sēstertius, exīstimō, mīstum* (*mīxtum*), *pīstum, pīstor, prīstinus, trīstis, ōstium, prōstellum, prōsternō, prōstibulum, crūstum, crūsta, frūstum, fūstis, jūstus, palūster, pūstula, rūsticus, ūstus.* Perhaps *vēstīgium, vēstibulum, dīstō, tōstum.* (See also Rule 9.)

str. *rāstrum, bimēstris, sēmēstris, pīstrīlla, pīstrinum, sīstrum, rōstrum, frūstra, lūstrō, lūstrum, inlūstris.*

(iii) Long vowels before various other consonant combinations.

ct. *lēctor, rēctor, plēctrum, vīctum* (*vīvō*), *frūctus* (*fruor*), *lūctus, rūctus, strūctum.* Perhaps *flūctus.* (See also Rules 2 and 12.)

gm. *āgmen, frāgmen, frāgmentum, prāgmaticus.*

ll. *mālle, vāllum, catēlla* (chain), *anguīlla, catīllus, bovīllus, fovīlla, mīlle, pīstrīlla, pulvīllus, stīlla, suīllus, vīlla, corōlla, ōlla, nōlle, ūllus, nūllus.* Probably also *favīlla, hīllae, ovīllus.* (Contrast *pălleo, vĕlle, vĕllo, pĕllo, patĕlla, tītĭllo, vĭllus, pŏlleo, pŭllus,* &c.)

lm. *pūlmō.*

ls. *sōlstitium* (see Rule 10). Probably also *ālsī, fūlsī, mūlsī* (mŭlgeo), *indūlsī* (note the **g** in the present indicative of these four perfects, and cf. Rule 2, note). (Contrast *fălsus, pŭlsus, vŭlsus, mŭlsī* (mŭlceo), &c.)

lt. *ūltimus, ūltrā*[1].

mb. *cōmbūrō*[2].

mn. *lāmna.*

mps. *dēmpsī, cōmpsī, prōmpsī, sūmpsī* (note the origin of the long vowel, in the present indicatives). (Contrast *contĕmpsī.*)

mpt. *dēmptus, cōmptus, prōmptus, sūmptus.* (Contrast *contĕmptus.*) There is doubt about *ēmptus* (co-*ēmptus, redēmptus,* &c.).

nc. *prīnceps, quīncunx, ūncia, sēmūncia.*

nct. *ūnctiō,* &c. (See Rule 3.)

nd. *prēndō* (for *pre-hendō*), *vēndō* (for *vēnum-dō*) (see § 77 (2) and § 79, II, 2), *nōndum, ūndecim, quīndecim, ūndēvīgintī, nūndinae, vīndēmia,* and possibly *frōndis*[3] (frōns). (But the vowel is generally short before this very common consonant combination: *amăndus, monĕndus, ŭndique,* &c.)

ng. *nōngentī.*

nn. *nōnne.*

nq. *quīnque, quīnquiēns, quīnquāgintā,* &c.

---

[1] Lewis. But both very doubtful. See Lindsay, p. 594, Stowasser, p. 760, and Heinichen, p. 602.

[2] Heinichen. (But very doubtful.) [3] See p. 54, footnote.

nt. *cōntiō* (for *cō-ventiō*), *nūntius* (*nūntiō*, &c.). (But before *nt* the vowel is nearly always short : *amănt*[1], *rēxissĕnt*, &c.)

nx. *quīncūnx, conjūnx.* (See also Rule 3.)

ps. *rēpsī, reāpse.* (See also Rule 4.)

pt. *scrīptor, rēptum, scēptrum, nūptiae, alīptēs.* (See also Rule 4.)

rc. *ōrca, sūrculus.* (See also Rule 6.)

rd. *ārdeō* (*ārdēscō*), *bārdus, lārdum, ōrdō, ōrdior, prīmōrdium.* (See also Rule 6.)

rg. *jūrgo, pūrgō* (*pūrgātiō*); and possibly *pērgō, expērgīscor.*

rm. *fōrma, fīrmus.* (See Rule 12.) (Contrast *fŏrmīdō, fŏrmīca.*)

rn. *vērnus, hōrnus, ōrnō,* and perhaps *ūrna.* (Contrast *supĕrnus,* &c.)

rp. *ūsūrpō.* (See Rule 12.)

rr. *nārrō.* (See Rule 12.)

rs. *ārsī, ārsūrus, ōrsus, hōrsum, intōrsum, intrōrsum, prōrsum, quōrsum, sinistrōrsus, rūrsum, sūrsum.* Probably also *spārsī, spārsum, mērsī, mērsum, tērsī, tērsum, conspērsī, conspērsum, ūrsī.* Possibly also *fōrs, fōrsit, mōrsum.* (But *tŏrsī, cŭrsum.*)

rt. *quārtus, fūrtim, fūrtum.* Possibly also *fōrte, fōrtāsse, fōrtūna, fōrtuĭtus.* (But *fŏrtitūdō, fŏrtiter,* &c.)

sq. *sēsquī.*

ss. *māssa, fŏrtāsse*[2]. (See also Rule 9.) Probably also *pāssum, cēssī, cēssum, sēssum, cōnsēssum, grēssus,*

---

[1] Roby has *amănt* (*Grammar*, Pt. I. p. 227) and *amănt* (*School Grammar*, p. 91); he also has *regĕnt* (*S. G.* p. 16) and *regĕnt* (*G.* I. p. 26, and *S. G.* p. 90). But in all verbal endings the vowel before *nt* is invariably short.

[2] Stowasser, Heinichen.

fĭssum, scĭssum, fŏssum (note the **d** in the pres.
indic. of these verbs); *mĭssum, ēsse* (eat), *jŭssī,
jŭssus, ūssī.*

tt. *mĭttō.*

x. See Rules 2, 3, 5 and 12; *rēxī, tēxī, dīxī, fīxī, -flīxī,
vīxī, dūxī, lūxī, flūxī, sūxī, fĭxum, lūxus, nīxus,
māximus.* Possibly also *trāxī, flēxī, -frīxī, rīxa.*
(But *allĕxī, nĕxī, pĕxī, vĕxī, cŏxī, strŭxī, flĕxum.*)

xt. *jūxta, mīxtum.*

(iv) A long vowel before two consonants is found in a
large number of proper names. Here are a few:

*Pūblicola, Sōcratēs, Āfrica, Iōlcus, Aquĭllius, Īllyria,
Pōllio, Lēmnos, Tēmnos, Clytēmnēstra, Mānlius,
Vīpsānius, Nōrba, Lycūrgus, Nārnia, Mārs, Lārs,
Crēssa, Thrēssa, Tartēssus, Telmēssus, Cnōssus,
Polymēstor, Sēstius, Sēstos, Ōstia, Prāxitelēs, Ōxus,
Rōxānē, Amāzōn[1].*

CHAPTER X

ACCENT

83. When, in English, we pronounce such a word as
economy, we are said to "accent" the second syllable, or, in
other words, to give that syllable a greater emphasis or
stress than the other three. But the precise nature of this

[1] Professor Sonnenschein objects to the recoguition, in ordinary practice,
of hidden quantities, mainly on the grounds of conflict of opinion, of insufficient evidence, and of unnecessary additional difficulty.—See *Proc. of
the Class. Assoc.*, Jan. 1912, pp. 87—92, and *Class. Rev.*, May 1912 and May
1913. See also Canon Sloman's reply in *Class. Rev.*, Nov. 1912, and
Professor Buck's reply in *Class. Rev.*, June 1913.

stress has never been satisfactorily analysed. To say that
it simply means additional "force" or "loudness" does not
seem entirely to meet the case. There is probably a further
element, that of musical pitch.

Everybody knows that the sound of a violin-string or of
a pianoforte-wire is due to vibrations brought about by
bowing and striking, respectively. If we tighten the string
or the wire, we increase the rapidity of the vibrations, with
the consequence that the *pitch* of the sound is raised. Similarly, the pitch of the human voice is raised by an increase
in the tension of the vocal chords.

When two notes from two different sources are of the
same pitch, their rates of vibration are the same. If a
tuning-fork, or a pianoforte-wire, or a violin-string, or an
organ-pipe, or a tongue of a concertina, all produce the same
note as the human voice, it is because the vibrations of the
tuning-fork, of the pianoforte-wire, of the string, of the air-
column, and of the tongue of the concertina, all vibrate at
the same rate as the vocal chords of the singer.

Changes of pitch in the human voice may proceed either
by *leaps* or by *glides*. In singing, the voice generally dwells
without change of pitch on each note, and leaps upwards or
downwards to the next note as quickly as possible. *The
differences of pitch are easily measured.* In speech, the
voice only occasionally dwells on one note and is constantly
moving from one note to the other, so that the different
notes are simply points between which the voice is con-
tinually gliding. *These differences of pitch are exceedingly
difficult to measure accurately.*

An absolutely *level* tone hardly ever occurs in speech.
An approach to the level tone may be heard in the word

well as an expression of musing or meditation. A "rising" intonation may be heard in questions or doubtful hesitating statements, as, *are you ready?* A "falling" intonation may be heard in answers, commands, or dogmatic assertions, as in *Yes, I am.* A "compound rise" may be heard in such a sentence as *take care!* when uttered warningly; a "compound fall" in *oh! oh really!* when implying sarcasm.

But in ordinary speech, the extent to which (if at all) pitch enters with stress into the so-called accent in accented syllables of English polysyllables, it is very difficult to say. It is this particular difficulty which creates much of the uncertainty which we feel in estimating the value of the available evidence in connection with accent and accentuation in Latin. Our knowledge of Latin accent is slight, authoritative evidence being meagre, but this has not prevented many well-known investigators from adopting a very dogmatic attitude on the subject. Many of their mistakes are due to misleading associations with the term accent as commonly used in connection with English.—Was the Latin "accent" one of pitch or of stress?

84. Of the musical character of *Greek* accent, there is no doubt at all. Dionysius of Halicarnassus makes this quite clear[1]. From him we learn that "the art of public speaking is a musical one too; for it differs from that used in songs and on instruments in quantity, not in quality. For in public speaking, words have also melody, rhythm, modulation and propriety. In speaking then also, the ear is delighted with melody, is impelled by the rhythm, and especially longs for propriety. The difference is merely one

[1] In a treatise περὶ συνθέσεως ὀνομάτων.

of degree. The melody of speech is measured by a single
musical interval which is as nearly as possible that called
a Fifth." And he proceeds to identify Greek accent with
pitch, and does so in explicit terms[1]. As Professor Postgate
points out[2], the limited influence of stress on Greek phonology
may well be due to the dominance of the pitch accent
which subsequently attracted it and was then absorbed
into it. In fact, there was, in course of time, a profound
change from pitch to stress, and the musical character of
accent seems to have disappeared altogether.

In *Latin* the problem is more difficult. A fifth century
grammarian remarks[3] that the accented syllable in a Latin
word is the syllable which could be heard at a distance
when the others were inaudible. This, however, tells us
little, though perhaps it suggests stress-accent rather than
pitch-accent. Yet there can be no doubt about the existence
of a pitch-accent, and Brugmann, amongst others, explicitly
recognises that musical accent was still alive in classical times.
In Roman speech, as in Greek speech, there appears to have
been a rise and fall of pitch, though this, of course, was a
gradual slide, and not a leap through an interval as in
singing[4]. And there is the clear and direct evidence of
authoritative Roman writers to the effect that, in what
they regarded as the accented syllable of words, there was

---

[1] For Ellis's translation, as corrected by Professor Postgate, see "Flaws
in Classical Research," *Proceedings of the British Academy*, 1907–8, pp.
184—5. Cf. Ellis, *Quan. Pron. of Latin*, pp. 27—29. (Dionysius also
clearly stated that there was a strict observance of quantity in prose.)

[2] *Classical Review*, 1899, *Notice* on Brugmann.

[3] Lindsay, *Latin Language*, pp. 17, 152.

[4] This is proved incidentally by Vitruvius, *Archit.* v. 4, translating
Aristoxenus (Postgate, *Class. Rev.* Vol. xix. p. 364 footnote).

a distinct rise of pitch. This evidence it is foolish to try to controvert, in spite of difficulties we may experience in explaining other phenomena of the Latin language. Take, for instance, the question of syncopated doublets[1], e.g., *solidum* and *soldum*. It is useless to try to prove from these that Latin accent was entirely a stress-accent, for, as Professor Postgate clearly shows[2], these doublets will be produced whether the accent is pitch or stress, and if rapid speaking shortens a word the qualitative predominance of the musical accent is just as effective a protection to its proper syllable as is the quantitative predominance of the stress-accent. True these doublets do tell us something about the syllables that lie outside the main accent. The syllable of weakened force went to the wall and a doublet sprang into being. Hence, when we see *solidum* syncopated to *soldum*, and *calidus* to *caldus*, we can infer that the syllable *li* was pronounced with less force than the respective final syllables *dum* and *dus*.

The educated pronunciation of Latin, at least so far as quantity was concerned, was powerfully influenced by the Greek, and no doubt in both languages there was a tendency for the pitch-accent gradually to give way to the stress-accent and ultimately to be lost in it. But there is nothing to show that, at least in classical times, differences of pitch and differences of stress were not absolutely independent. They *may* not have been, but our positive knowledge of the whole subject is of the slightest, and the delimitation of pitch-accent and stress-accent is a matter which investigators have still to determine.

---

[1] See Postgate, *Class. Phil.* Vol. III. No. 1, pp. 99—100, and note 2 *ante*.

[2] *Ib.* Cf. Lindsay, *op. cit.* p. 150. Cf. also Professor C. Exon's views in *Hermathena* for 1908, pp. 202 foll.

It is true that ancient writers on Latin grammar were
seldom Romans by birth and that they were usually Greeks,
and no doubt, as Mr Lindsay says, the latter would have
the same difficulty in describing the Latin accent as a
Frenchman in describing the strong accent in English. But
the explicit testimony of the ancient writers, considered
as a whole, must stand first; and modern inferences from
apparent inconsistencies of language, second. That the two
things are at present frequently in conflict there is no doubt,
but when a reconciliation between them takes place, there is
certainly a balance of probability that the former will prove
to have been right and the latter wrong. Would those who
argue to the contrary accept from Macaulay's New Zealander
an English essay of a twentieth century school boy, or a
cockney coster song, which he had unearthed in forgotten
London, as evidence to controvert Sweet's statements about
the present-day spelling and pronunciation of English ?

Not the least of our difficulties is to decide precisely
what the ancient writers *meant* when they used the term
"pitch" in connection with accent in speech. Of the nature
of this pitch as they used it in their own spoken language
they were, presumably, at least as ill-informed as we are
of the nature of pitch in our own. Present-day phonetic
experts are by no means agreed as to the relative pitch of
the different syllables when we pronounce such a word as
economy. One well-known authority thinks that pitch and
stress are absolutely independent and that in every word
the syllable of highest pitch is the first, while other competent authorities maintain that the stressed syllable of a
word is always the one of highest (or lowest) pitch. The
point has not yet been experimentally determined satisfactorily, and hence rival hypotheses prevail. Once we

begin to dwell, as in singing, on a particular syllable of a spoken word, the pitch is changed almost unconsciously. Correct measurement is thus very difficult, though ultimately the phonograph may help us to solve the problem[1].

On the whole question the opinion now prevails that when, if ever, the facts which bear upon the case are duly ascertained and co-ordinated, the probability is that the outcome will be something like the following:—The separate syllables of independent words in Latin had uniformity neither of pitch nor of stress. The syllable which received the greatest force might be the one which had the highest pitch or it might not. From the variation arose, especially in the earlier period, fluctuations and anomalies of quantity, as, for example, syllables which were neither short nor long in the strict sense, and syllables with different quantity in different forms of the same word. Under Greek influences, these variations were reduced until there was an approximation to a condition of nearly uniform stress. The preponderant stress (the "main" stress-accent) in the case of polysyllables tended in the time of which we know anything to move toward the end of the word, though it never passed beyond the second syllable from the end, and thus to coincide with the main pitch-accent. It was not till after this movement was completed that the joint-accent lost its musical character and survived as a stress-accent alone[2].

[1] From phonographic records, it seems to be an established fact that when the voice is tired, differences of pitch are much less than when the voice is fresh and vigorous. On the remarkable differences of pitch in Chinese speech, consult any educated Chinaman on speech "tones." See also *Bibliography*, Vol. 43.

[2] *Accent in Latin, Class. Phil.* Vol. III. No. 1.

85. There is general agreement about one point, and that is that the very marked stress given to accented syllables in English and German was quite unknown in Latin. On the other hand, there was something of a more definite nature than is found in French, where the even gliding over the different syllables of words sometimes makes it difficult to distinguish any accent whatever except at the extreme end of a sentence[1].

In practice the accepted rules are:

(i) Accented syllables in Latin must be pronounced much more gently than accented syllables in English.

(ii) Unaccented syllables in Latin must not be rapidly slurred over as is so often the case in English. Particular attention must be paid to the proper length of every syllable. An unaccented long syllable takes just as much *time* to pronounce as an accented long syllable, *and twice as much time as an accented short syllable.* There must, in fact, be a much more even distribution of force over the syllables of a Latin word than in English, and the accent must never be allowed to destroy the proper length of the unaccented syllables.

(iii) No conscious attempt must be made to pitch the accented syllable in a higher key. The usual (and unconscious) difference of pitch supposed (by some authorities) to exist in ordinary English speech will suffice.

[1] Latin accent gives much trouble to French speakers.—"Chi non ha sentito leggere da un francese uno squarcio di Virgilio, non può immaginare che scempio si possa fare degli accenti e per conseguenza del ritmo di versi tanto armoniosi."—*Riv. di Fil. e d'Istr. Class.* xliv. ii.

It must not be thought that, because there was possibly a fixed difference of pitch between accented and unaccented syllables, there was in Roman speech anything of the nature of chanting. That Virgil in reading the Aeneid would make his hearers conscious of other musical qualities than mere rhythm there can be no doubt, and it is possible that, in poetry, chanting of some form usually if not always took the place of reading; but it requires considerable imagination to think of Cicero intoning his political and forensic orations. There was probably at least as much *modulation* of voice in the case of Roman orators as in the case of the best speakers of the present day.

86. In what follows no distinction is made between the "acute" and the "circumflex" accent. If due attention be paid to the proper length of syllables and of vowels, especially of vowels in final syllables, it is unnecessary to distinguish between the two kinds of accent. At all events the only other distinction, that of rising and falling pitch, is probably outside the range of the possible practice of any but a few experts.

Position of the Accent.

I. **General Rules:**

(1) **Words of two syllables are accented on the first:** *dŭrō, mḗnsă, bŏnīs, mŏdŏ, fŏrtĕ.*

(2) **Words of more than two syllables are accented**

(a) **On the last syllable but one (the penult) if that is long**[1]: *lēgátī, nātúră, ămábās, ămárĕ,*

---

[1] It has already been pointed out (§ 67 *et seq.*) that a long syllable often contains a short vowel.

ĭngĕntēs, măgĭstĕr, ĕxpăndŭnt, cŏmpĕrtŭm, lātĭtādō, hŏrtābŭntŭr, ămābămŭs, dēbĭlĭtārĕ.

(b) **On the last syllable but two (the antepenult) if the penult is short**: *nátĭō, cŏmprĭmō, plĕtās, cápĭĕnt, quómŏdŏ, rĕgĕrĕt, lăcrĭmă, vŏlŭcrĭs, tĕnĕbrae, mŏllĭssĭmae, ŏffĕndĕrĕ, ămávĕrō, mŏnŭĕrās, pŏtŭĕrăm, hŏrtārĕmĭnĭ, nĭhĭlómĭnŭs.*

II. Subsidiary Rules:

(1) Compounds are accented according to the general rules, no matter whether their parts can be used as separate words or not: *ádfĕrō, cónfĭcĭt, tĕrrĭgĕnă, ádmŏdŭm, ănhélŭs, pŏstmŏdŏ, rēspúblĭcă* (or *rés públĭcă*).

But in non-prepositional compounds of *făcĭō*, such as *călĕfăcĭō, tĕpĕfăcĭō, bĕnĕfăcĭō, mānsuĕfăcĭō* (which were originally written in separate parts), the accent is always on the verb; thus *călĕfăcĭt* (not *călĕfăcĭt*); so in the passive,—*călĕfít*, &c. But prepositional compounds follow the general rule: *áffĭcĭt, cónfĭcĭt*, &c.

(2) Sometimes a final syllable following a long penult is lost, or there is contraction. In such cases the accent is retained on the syllable which has now become final.

(a) Adjectives in *-ās (-ātĭs)* denoting one's native place. The original form was *-ātĭs* which was contracted to *-āts* and then to *-ās*: *Maecēnás, Arpīnás, Lārīnás*; so also *nŏstrás, vĕstrás, prīmás*.

(*b*) Shortened perfects of the fourth conjugation: *audĭt* (for *audívĭt*), *mūnít*, *pĕtít*, *ŏbít.*

(*c*) Shortened imperatives: *ăddúc* (for *ăddūcĕ*), *prodúc, benedíc.*

(*d*) Shortened demonstratives: *ĭllíc* (for *ĭllícĕ*), *ĭstíc.*

(*e*) Similarly *tăntón* (for *tăntónĕ*), *sătín* (*sătísnĕ*), *audín* (*audísnĕ*), *vĭdén* (for *vĭdén, vĭdésnĕ*), *pŏtín* (*pŏtísnĕ*), *ăntĕhác* (*ăntĕhácĕ*), &c. So "*Pўrrhín* connubia seruas" (Virg. *Aen.* 3. 319).

(3) The Genitives and Vocatives in *i* of nouns in *-ius* preserve their accent as if they retained their endings in *ii* and *ie*; thus the accent appears on a short penult: *Vĭrgílĭ* (for *Vĭrgílĭĭ* and *Vĭrgílĭĭ*), *Ŏvĭdī, Mĕrcúrī, Vălĕrī.* So *ĭngĕnī* (for *ĭngĕnĭĭ*).

(4) The enclitics *-que*, *-ne*, *-ve*, *-ce* displace the accent and attract it to the final syllable of the words to which they are joined[1]. Thus *hŏmĭnŭm*, but *hŏmĭnŭmquĕ; ĭllī* but *ĭllícĕ; dĕŭs* but *dĕúsvĕ; cŭnctă* but *cŭnctănĕ?*

So with *-met*, *-pte*, and *-dum*: thus, *ĕgŏ* but *ĕgŏmĕt; nŏstră* but *nŏstrăptĕ; rĕspĭcĕ* but *rĕspĭcĕdŭm.*

And with the separable words *inde* and *quando*: thus, *ĕxĭndĕ* (not *ĕxĭndĕ*); *ĕcquăndō* (not *ĕcquăndō*).

(5) Such words as *lĭbĕt*, *lĭcĕt* and *quĭdĕm* are sometimes called enclitics, since, like enclitics proper, they may be attached to other words. But in such cases, owing to their own quantity, the accent is

---

[1] But in early Latin such forms were accented according to the general rule. Thus *bŏnă, bŏnăquĕ; lĭmĭnă, lĭmĭnăquĕ.* And some authorities think that this practice obtained even later.

the same whether they be considered as enclitics proper or as parts of a compound: *quĭbŭslĭbĕt, scĭlĭcĕt, quăndŏ́quĭdĕm* or *quăndŏ́quĭdĕm.* So with *quăntŭ́mvīs.*

(6) In certain words the particle *-que* has become inseparable; it is no longer a conjunction and is therefore no longer an enclitic. Hence the accent follows the general rule: *dénĭquĕ, ĭtăquĕ, ŭtĭquĕ, ŭndĭquĕ.*

But in some of these cases the *-que* may still occasionally do duty as an enclitic. Hence

ĭtăquĕ = and so; *ĭtăquĕ* = therefore.

ŭtĭquĕ = and as; *ŭtĭquĕ* = in any case.

(7) Throughout the declension of *ŭtĕ́rquĕ*, the accent falls on the penult. Thus we have not only *ŭtĕ́rquĕ* and *ŭtrŭ́mquĕ* (according to rule), but also *ŭtrăquĕ.* (Cf. Rule 4.) So with *plērŭ́squĕ, plērăquĕ, plērŭ́mquĕ.*

(8) Prepositions are seldom accented or stressed[1] in any way, even in English; and in Latin when immediately preceding their nouns they lose their accent altogether. For all practical purposes a preposition may be regarded as compounded with its following noun. Thus *pĕr hŏstēs* is not *pĕ́r hŏstēs* but *pĕr*

---

[1] We may be said to "accent" a *syllable* of a word, but the additional force given to a word as a whole is usually known as "stress" (in French, "oratorical accent"). Hence, although the term "accent," as ordinarily used, is hardly applicable to monosyllables, many monosyllables naturally receive stress or oratorical accent, according to the subject and the speaker. But words like prepositions and conjunctions are less likely than any other words to receive stress in ordinary speech.

hŏstēs; sŭprā mŏntĕm is not *sŭprā mŏntĕm* but *sŭprā mŏntĕm*. They are not, however, real compounds. Although the preposition generally loses its accent altogether, some authorities favour *ăpŭd mē* and *ĭntĕr nos*.

If, however, a preposition follows its noun it retains its own accent: *tĕ sĭnĕ, quácŭm, quáeprŏpter*.

But *cŭm* after a personal pronoun is enclitic: thus *nōbtscŭm, vōbtscŭm*.

(9) Conjunctions beginning a phrase do not take an accent; but if not beginning a phrase they are accented according to general rule: *sĕd Gállĭ, sĭ quĭd vĕllĕnt*; but *tá quŏquĕ, vós ĭgĭtŭr*.

(10) The relative is unaccented, the interrogative accented: *quō dĭē rĕdĭĭt* (on which day he returned); *quó dĭē?* (on which day?).

(11) The accent in the case of many words of the type mentioned in § 66 (4) (5) varies. The normal pronunciation is *lă-tĕ-bră, mă-nĭ-plŭs*, &c. But when, as is often the case in poetry, the consonant combinations are divided in order to lengthen the preceding syllable, the pronunciation is *lă-tĕb-ră, mă-nĭp-lŭs*[1]. In such words as *ăgrĭcŏlă* and

---

[1] i.e. the mute is pronounced with the preceding vowel, adding a unit of time. Contrast the division of the word *latebras* in the two following lines:

| aut | te-re- | brā- | re ca- | vā- | su-te- | rĭ et | temp | tā- | re la- | teb- | rās. | *Aen.* 2. 38 |
| tum | le-vis | haut | ul- | trā | la-te- | brās | jam | quae- | ri-ti- | mā- | gō. | *Aen.* 10. 663 |

In the same verse Horace has *nig-ris, ni-groque*; Ovid, *volu-cri, voluc-ris*; Virgil, *pa-tris, pat-rem*; Lucretius, *pa-tribus, pat-res.*

pătrĭs, the division of the consonant combination although changing the length of the syllable cannot, of course, affect the accent[1]; thus *ă-grĭ-cŏ-lă* and *ăg-rĭ-cŏ-lă; pă-trĭs* and *păt-rĭs*. (It has already been pointed out that in these cases the length and the pronunciation of the vowel remains unaltered. *It is the syllable, not the vowel, that is lengthened.*)

(12) The pronunciation of the pronominal genitives in *-ius* may also vary. (See § 79, II, Exception *a.*) Thus we may have *ĭl-lĭ-ŭs* or *ĭl-lĭ-ŭs; tō-tĭ-ŭs* or *tŏ-tĭ-ŭs.*

(13) It is probable that, as in English, words of more than three syllables frequently had a second, though lighter accent; and even a third in the case of very long words: thus *ăpplĭcărĕ, măgnĭtúdō, nōbĭlĭtátĭs, ĕxĕrcĭtătĭónĭbŭs.*

(14) The first part of a compound especially may have retained to some extent the accent which it had as a single word: *nĭhĭlómĭnŭs, ănĭmădvĕrtō.*

If, however, the English practice is at all closely imitated, the shortening of long syllables is inevitable, and it has to be remembered that, in Latin, correct syllable length is of fundamental importance.

---

[1] Since in the case of *agricola*, the penult is short with either method of division; the antepenult therefore takes the accent; in the case of *patris*, the accent must in either case fall on the first syllable. (But this does not, of course, apply to such a word as *tenebras*, the normal pronunciation of which is *ténebras*, but, when a long penult is required, *tenĕb-ras.*—See Quint. I. 5. 28.)

CHAPTER XI

GENERAL REMARKS ON QUANTITY AND ACCENT

87. Certain faults are as common in the "restored Roman" (the "new") pronunciation as in the "English" (the "old") pronunciation of Latin. They are principally,

(1) The shortening of long vowels in all unaccented syllables.

(2) The shortening of all long syllables which are not accented.

(3) The lengthening of short vowels in accented syllables.

These faults are such as naturally result from our English habits of speaking. The heavy English accent tends, necessarily, to lengthen the accented syllable of a word and to shorten the other syllables.

88. It is a very common thing for a classical teacher to accept as correct the pronunciation of, for example, such a word as *ămāvérŭnt*, provided that the *e* is pronounced long and is accented, the difference in the length of the *ă* and the *ā* and the proper length of the last syllable of the word receiving no attention whatever. It is not pointed out that the last three syllables of the word are of equal length and that they take equal periods of time to pronounce. Thus it comes about that as soon as a boy is introduced to verse he has to face a number of "new rules" concerning quantity, rules which appear to him to be largely artificial ; whereas if he had been taught to read prose in the proper way, most of these "new rules" would be entirely unnecessary, and he would discover the musical rhythm of the verse almost unconsciously.

The word *sŏcĭĕtās* illustrates the last of the three faults mentioned in § 87. A beginner is rightly expected to accent the syllable *cĭ*, but the chances are about even that if he does not bring out a long clear English *i*[1] he will be reprimanded for not paying proper attention to his quantities! It is a rare thing to hear such a word pronounced correctly,— with the fourth syllable given twice the time of any one of the three others, and with the vowels in the short syllables given their correct phonetic length.

89. Typical words of two, three, and four syllables will now be taken and their pronunciation illustrated by means of English words. The English words are carefully selected in order to represent, as far as possible, the relative length of the syllables in the Latin words. A short Latin syllable will, for example, be illustrated by an English word containing a short vowel, usually **i** or **e** or **y**, simply because such a word is most suggestive of shortness. In a similar way, an English word containing a long **a, o**, or **u**, or a diphthong, sometimes followed by one or more consonants, will be made to represent the Latin long syllable. Illustrative words of this kind are a great help in attuning the ear to accuracy of quantity in a succession of syllables.

90. Words of two syllables. It is obvious that as there are "long" and "short" syllables, we may have four types of Latin words of two syllables, viz., a word of two long syllables, one long syllable followed by one short, one

[1] i.e. the diphthong heard in such English words as *society*, *finally*.

short followed by one long, and two short. These may be conveniently named after the so-called "feet" in Latin, viz.,

The **Spondee** (– –) as in *cōgī*.
The **Trochee** (– ⏑)   „   *cūră*.
The **Iambus** (⏑ –)   „   *gĕnū*.
The **Pyrrhic** (⏑ ⏑)   „   *bĕnĕ*.

But it is misleading to use the vowel marks (– and ⏑) to represent *syllable* length, seeing that a long syllable often contains a short vowel. The marks will therefore only be used to represent vowel-length. Syllable lengths will be represented by musical notes, a long syllable by a crotchet (♩) and a short syllable by a quaver (♪)[1].

91. (1) The *Spondee* (♩♩): **cōgī**, **īrae**, **hōrtōs**, **prū-dēns**. The relative syllable lengths may be obtained by imitating, quantitatively, the pronunciation of the English words *boar-hound*. These words illustrate the case better than, say, the words *tall girl*, for the word *boar* takes a slight accent, whereas in the second case the slight accent falls on the word *girl*. Yet the word *hound* takes as much time to pronounce as the word *boar*.—The tendency with this type is to shorten the second syllable, a tendency which must be carefully guarded against.

[1] The crotchet and quaver are intended to represent *time* periods only. It may, however, be mentioned that some authorities write the accented syllable of a word a perfect fifth above the unaccented syllable.   Thus :

ă - mā - vē - runt

There is not sufficient justification for this in Latin, though there is in Greek.

(2) The *Trochee* (♩♪): cúră, cắstă, rēgĕ, mílĕ. For relative time, compare such English words as *houses* or *fairy*. This is a very easy type. Care must, however, be taken to prevent the final short vowel from becoming the indefinite vowel sound referred to in § 9.

(3) The *Iambus* (♪♩): bŏnīs, mĕī, ămō, gĕnū. For relative time compare such English words as *sinews* or *volume*. No type is more difficult than this. The first syllable though accented must be kept short, and the second must be made long. No fault is more common in Latin pronunciation than to convert an iambus into a trochee: thus bŏnīs is often incorrectly pronounced bŏnĭs; sŭīs, sŭĭs; ămō, ămŏ; and so on. Indeed, such words as sŭīs and mĕī are difficult to pronounce even approximately accurately.

(4) The *Pyrrhic* (♪♪): bĕnĕ, pĭă, căpră, prŏpĕ. For relative time compare such English words as *river* or *money*. Here again it is necessary to guard against lengthening the accented syllable. The above words are frequently pronounced incorrectly, as bēnĕ, pĭă, cāpră, prōpĕ. So with all Pyrrhics, so-called.

The somewhat common practice of allowing boys to say their declensions and conjugations with the accent on the last syllable of the word leads to faults that are probably seldom quite eradicated afterwards. The accent is, of course, *never* on the final syllable in the ordinary cases of declensions and conjugations.

Contrast also ămō (♪♩) with ămăt (♪♪); bŏnŭs (♪♪) with bŏnīs (♪♩); mēnsă (♩♪) with mēnsā (♩♩); hŏstīs (♩♪) with hŏstēs (♩♩); &c.

92. Words of three syllables. It is obvious that as each of the four types of dissyllables just mentioned may be preceded by another syllable either long or short, there are, as regards syllable length, eight types of words of three syllables. The following table shows (*a*) their metrical names (which are used here merely for purposes of reference); (*b*) their time periods; (*c*) illustrative Latin words; and (*d*) English words to illustrate as closely as possible the time periods.

(1) Molossus.	♩ ♩ ♩	nōlītō,	cŏllīdĕnt,	"slow boar-hound."
(2) Bacchius.	♪ ♩ ♩	rĕpōnō,	rĕtārdănt,	"cigar-box."
(3) Palimbacchius.	♩ ♩ ♪	nātūră,	sēmēntĭs[1],	"great horses."
(4) Amphibrach.	♪ ♩ ♪	cŏrōnă,	părēntĭs,	"remainder."
(5) Cretic.	♩ ♪ ♩	cīvĭtās,	cărpĕrĕnt,	"vulpicide."
(6) Anapaest.	♪ ♪ ♩	lăpĭdēs,	mŏnĕănt,	"pinafore."
(7) Dactyl.	♩ ♪ ♪	lămĭnă,	cŏmpŏtĭs,	"juniper."
(8) Tribrach	♪ ♪ ♪	făcĕrĕ,	lăcrĭmă,	"dimity."

Note that the accent is on the penult in the first four cases, and on the antepenult in the last four.

No. 1 (the Molossus) is difficult. Careless speakers shorten the first and last syllables and convert the Molossus into an Amphibrach (no. 4).

No. 2 is also rather difficult. The third syllable must be made as long as the second.

In no. 3 there is a general tendency to shorten the first syllable.

---

[1] With respect to the length of final syllables, see § 70.

No. 4 is easy; so is no. 7.

In no. 5 care must be taken to make the last syllable long. So with no. 6.

The first syllable of no. 7 should be compared with that of no. 8. Note that it is twice as long.

It is good practice to pronounce the suggested English words first, and then to pronounce the Latin words in as nearly as possible the same time, and with a similar rhythm.

93. Words of four syllables. Any one of the eight types of trisyllables may be preceded by another syllable, either long or short.   There are thus sixteen kinds of words of four syllables, all differently constituted as regards syllable length.   The following examples[1] should be carefully pronounced in conjunction with the suggested English words.

(1) ♩ ♩ ♩ ♩ ōrātŏ́rēs, dēfĕndĭ́ssĕnt, "our   slow   boarhound."

(2) ♪♩ ♩ ♩ rĕcūsā́vī, cŭcŭrrĕ́rŭnt, "the   slow   boarhound."

(3) ♩ ♪♩ ♩ ēlăbŏ́rō,   cŏncĭtā́rī,   "new cigar-box."

(4) ♪ ♪♩ ♩ vĕnĕrā́rī, mŏnŭĭ́ssĕnt, "the cigar-box."

(5) ♩ ♩ ♩ ♪ nōlītŏ́tĕ,   cŏmmūtā́rĕ, "our white horses."

(6) ♪♩ ♩ ♪ cŏrōnā́rĕ, ămāvĭ́stĭs,   "the white horses."

(7) ♩ ♪♩ ♪ lītĭgā́tŏr,   ăpplĭcā́rĕ,   "no remainder."

(8) ♪ ♪♩ ♪ ănĭmā́rĕ,   vŏlŭĭ́ssĕm,   "inelastic."

(9) ♩ ♩ ♪♩ hērédĭtās, mŏllĭ́ssĭmae, "mean vulpicide."

---

[1] The names of the corresponding metrical feet are not given; they are hardly necessary and probably very few people ever trouble to learn them. If required they can be found in any good Latin grammar.

(10) ♪♩ ♪♩ sĕvĕrĭtās, ămávĕrănt,   "the vulpicide."

(11) ♩♪♩ fūtĭlĭtās, pĕrpĕtŭō,   "white pinafore."

(12) ♪♪♩ cĕlĕrĭtās, mŏnŭĕrĭs,   "the pinafore."

(13) ♩♩♪♪ mīrábĭlĕ, ĭntĕrprĕtĭs,   "fine juniper."

(14) ♪♩ ♪♪ pĕcūnĭă, ămábĕrĭs,   "the juniper."

(15) ♩♪♪♪ mātĕrĭă, ĭmprímĕrĕ,   "white dimity."

(16) ♪♪♪♪ mĕmóríă, quădrŭpĕdĕ,   "celerity."

Most of these require a great deal of practice. Particular
attention should be given to all unaccented long syllables.

It is useful to compare no. 11 of this section with no. 1
of the last section. The words **nōlítō** and **fūtílĭtās** are
pronounced in exactly the same time. The two intermediate syllables of the latter word take just as long to
pronounce as the middle syllable of the former. This should
be practised with the metronome or with the pendulum.
Other similar exercises may be devised; e.g., **mĕmóríă** is
pronounced in exactly the same time as **dīcō** [1].

94. If words of two, three, and four syllables are
correctly pronounced, words of more than four syllables need
cause little difficulty. A few examples are appended, together with English words suggestive of relative length.

(1) ♩♩♩♩♩ ĕxplōrātórēs,   "bright-eyed young boar-
                                         hound."

(2) ♩♪♪♩♪ nōbĭlĭtátĭs,   "hastily spoken."

(3) ♪♩♩♪♩ mŏnērémĭnī,   "a mean vulpicide."

(4) ♪♪♩ ♪♪ nĭhĭlōmĭnŭs,   "inebriety."

---

[1] So is a word like *fácĭlĭŭs*, an alternative accentuation for *făcĭlĭŭs*. This
very exceptional accentuation is supported by evidence of old Latin dramatic
verse, also of Ciceronian clausulae.

(5) ♪♩♩♪♪   tăbĕrnắcŭlŭm,
                 "the green juniper."

(6) ♩♪♩♩♪   cŏllăbōrắrĕ,
                 "eighty young horses."

(7) ♩♪♩♩♩♪   māchĭnāmĕntốrŭm,
                 "eighty-eight young horses."

(8) ♩♪♪♩♪♪♩   ĭnnŭmĕrābĭlĭtās,
                 "stain on a white pinafore."

(9) ♩♩♩♪♩♩♪♩♪   ĭncōnsĭdĕrātĭssĭmắrŭm[1],
                 "Gray bought forty old Roman vases."

95. As already stated, it is good practice to pronounce in immediate succession pairs of words which are closely akin as regards complete "time-periods." Compare, for instance, the word **ĕxplōrātōrēs** and the word **ĭnnŭmĕrābĭlĭtās.**

♩	♩	♩	♩	♩
ĕx	plō	rā	tố	rēs
ĭn	nŭ mĕ	rā	bĭ lĭ	tās
♪	♫	♪	♫	♪

Obviously the two words have equal time-periods, and the pronunciation should be practised with the metronome or pendulum. Monotone is preferable at first, in order that the short syllables may be given exactly half the length of the long syllables; at this stage the accent can be neglected.

[1] In these examples, secondary accents have been ignored. See § 86 ɪɪ (13).

Now pronounce, in time with the metronome, the English words suggested in § 94 (1) and (8), and note how the accents fall naturally on the word *boar* and *pin-*[1]. There ought now to be no difficulty in pronouncing the Latin words so that each syllable receives its correct amount of time and so that the accent falls in its proper place. *But the accent must be a very light accent.* The one important thing is *time.* Our English " sledge hammer " accent (as it has been so aptly called) must be avoided, and our slovenly English habit of " rushing " all unaccented syllables must also be avoided

CHAPTER XII

PROSE AND VERSE.—ACCENT AND ICTUS

96. The previous chapters have dealt mainly with the pronunciation of single words, and we now come to the differences between prose and verse. These differences, in Latin as in English, are characteristic, though they are by no means of the same type in the two languages. But before it is possible to deal adequately with the question of the pronunciation of Latin, as affected, if at all, by verse, it is necessary to touch upon the structure of English verse.

97. The chief respect in which verse differs from prose is in its regular succession of accented and unaccented syllables. This regularity of accent is called *rhythm.* Prose passages are, however, often rhythmical [2]:

[1] See footnote on previous page.

[2] The usual convention has been adopted of indicating the accented syllable of a word by placing the accent mark over the contained vowel, or, in the case of a diphthongal combination, over the second vowel of the combination.

"The Dóg-star and Aldébarán, poínting to the rést-
less Pleíadés, were hálf-way úp the Soúthern ský, and
betweén them húng Oríon, which górgeous cónstellátion
néver búrnt more vívidly than nów….The bárren and
gloómy Squáre of Pégasús was creéping roúnd to the
nórth-wést; fár awáy throúgh the plantátion, Véga
spárkled líke a lámp suspénded amíd the leáfless
treés."—*Far from the Madding Crowd.*

"They móved so géntly thát their foótsteps máde
no noíse, but thére were sóbs amóng the groúp and
soúnds of griéf and moúrning. For shé was deád.
Thére upón her líttle béd she láy at rést. The sólemn
stíllness wás no márvel nów. Where wére the tráces
of her eárly cáres, her súfferings and fatígues?—Áll
góne.—But peáce and pérfect háppinéss were bórn,
ímaged ín her tránquil beáuty and profoúnd repóse."—
The Old Curiosity Shop[1].

Now with these passages compare the following:

"Brought fróm the woóds, the hóneysúckle twínes
aroúnd the pórch, and seéms in thát trim pláce a plánt

---

[1] This passage from Dickens, though useful here for illustrating the
point in question, is rather a shocking specimen of prose rhythm. It was a
common fault of Dickens to write in this fashion: he constantly fell into
'metre.' Even in the first quoted passage, there is more than a suspicion
of metre, but Mr Hardy, like all good writers, reserves such usage for
exceptional occasions, and to the ear the result is not only unoffending but
is wholly pleasing. Rhythm, whether in prose or in verse, is essentially a
recurrence of some kind of unit of length, but whereas in verse the unit is
a metrical foot and therefore easily defined, in prose it is more arbitrary,
follows no rule, and cannot be defined in specific terms, though even in
prose the succession of units is sufficiently uniform to be suggestive of
regularity. Many admirable examples of prose rhythm may be found in the
Bible, e.g., Psalm xcvi., Eccl. iii. 1—8, and especially 1 Cor. xiii.—See chap. ix
of Professor Brewster's *The Writing of English.*

no lónger wíld; the cúltured róse there blóssoms, stróng
in heálth, and wíll be soón roof-hígh; the wíld pink
crówns the gárden wáll, and wíth the flówers are ínter-
míngled stónes spárry and bríght, rough scátterings óf
the hílls."—*The Excursion.*

This passage, although rhythmical like the first two, differs
from them in that it may be easily and naturally marked
off in lines of equal length. We thus have the following
arrangement, constituting " verse " :

> " Brought fróm the woóds, | the hóneysúckle twínes
> Aroúnd the pórch, | and seéms in thát trim pláce
> A plánt no lónger wíld ; | the cúltured róse
> There blóssoms, stróng in heálth, | and wíll be soón
> Roof-hígh ; | the wíld pink crówns the gárden wáll,
> And wíth the flówers are íntermíngled | stónes
> Spárry and bríght, | rough scátterings óf the hílls."

In reading either prose or verse, a frequent *pause* is necessary ; in order to breathe, the utterance is checked. In
verse the pause takes place at regular intervals. The length
of a line of poetry does not necessarily determine the length
of a sentence, but it usually does determine the length of a
phrase, for there is a natural tendency to pause at the end
of a complete line. If the line be long, a reader also pauses at
some other place, usually in or near the middle of the line. In
the above lines from Wordsworth, the bars indicate the pauses.

98. The rhythmical arrangement of words measured
off in lines of regular length is known as *metre.*

When reading verse the succession of accented syllables
seems to mark it off in equal steps; if marching, our feet
would keep time with them. Hence, as many syllables as can
be grouped about a clearly accented syllable is termed a *foot.*

The foot is the unit of metre. It usually consists of a group of either two or three syllables, one of which is accented. A *verse* is a cycle of feet forming a line of poetry.

The number of feet in a line determines its metre. We thus have the terms *tetrameter, pentameter, hexameter,* &c. The following are examples of tetrameters:

1. *Trochaic:*   Téll me | nót in | móurnful | númbers |
2. *Iambic:*   Unwépt | unhón- | oured ánd | unsúng |
3. *Dactylic:*   Óver the | roádways and | ón through the | víllages |
4. *Amphibrachic:* The flésh was | a pícture | for paínters | to stúdy |
5. *Anapaestic*[1]: O'er the lánd | of the frée | and the hóme | of the bráve |

99. In verse, the term *accent* is ambiguously used. Sometimes it refers to the stressed syllable in the standard pronunciation of a word (in this sense it is used in the previous chapters), and sometimes to the marked pulse-beat which the ear easily detects in the same place of each metrical foot in a verse. For the latter, however, the term *ictus* is often employed, and will be so employed in what follows here. In other words, *ictus* will denote *metrical* stress, while *accent* will denote the stress given to a particular syllable of a word according to the standard pronunciation.

In the above lines from Wordsworth the marks indicate the ictus, which, of course, falls on the second syllable of all the thirty-five iambic feet. In all the feet save one, ictus is identical with accent. The exception is the first foot of the last line; in the word *sparry,* the accent is on the first syllable, though the metrical stress (the ictus) is on the second.

---

[1] These terms will be understood from §§ 90, 91.

100.   A great deal of modern poetry is written in feet of a varying character.   This is a great relief to the reader who soon tires of symmetrical verses of the " half-up, half-down " type.   Here is an example (the bars indicate the feet):

> " Thére be | nóne of | Beaúty's | daúghters |
> With a má|gic like thée, |
> Ánd like | músic | ón the | wáters |
> Is thý | sweet voíce | to mé" | [1]

Variety is also frequently obtained by giving the ictus to unaccented syllables, or, to speak more correctly, by *accento rubato*.   Thus, translated into quantitative terms, the first of the following quotations gives us $- \smile \mid \smile -$|, and the fourth, $\smile \smile \mid --$|, the total length of the two feet taken together being in each case normal.   Similarly, the total ictus in the two feet taken together is normal[2].

(1)   " Státes*man* | with sleép-|less wátch | and steád-|fast aím." |
                                             —Ingram.

(2)   " And wíld | ró*ses* | and í-| vy sér-| pentíne."—*Shelley.*

(3)   " That thoú, | dead córse, | agaín | in *com-*| pléte steél." |
                                              —Shakespeare.

(4)   " To *fór-*| give wróngs | dárk*er* | than deáth | or níght." |
                                              —Shelley.

The unaccented syllables taking the ictus are shown in italics.   Sometimes the ictus falls upon a word which, from the sense of the passage, certainly ought not to be stressed; but although a good reader may almost—perhaps quite—ignore the ictus, he will make his hearers conscious of an ictus compensation:

1.   " Calm *ánd* | still líght | on yón | great plaín." | *—Tennyson.*

2.   " Land *óf* | the moún-| tain ánd | the floód." | *—Scott.*

---

[1] Metricians differ in opinion about the pointing of this last line.

[2] This distribution and compensation of ictus may be spread over a whole line, and allows of almost infinite variation.

101.   In the great majority of metrical feet in English poetry, ictus and accent fall together. But where they do not fall together, a good reader will never sacrifice accent to ictus,—if he did he would nullify the poet's intention, which is to avoid tiring the ear by a too monotonous sing-song. Nevertheless, a good reader always seems to make his audience conscious of both ictus and accent, the ictus being only *just* heard, however, and clearly subordinated to the accent   The natural accentual characteristic of every word is thus preserved, the swing of the metrical feet being at the same time gently indicated. Both are easily detected on the stage.

We may now return to the consideration of Latin. But it is desirable to point out that there is only a very faint similarity between the construction of English verse and the construction of Latin verse. The preceding remarks on English verse are in the main intended to prepare the reader for essential *points of difference*, not points of similarity, between English and Latin verse construction. It is quite true that, even in English, we cannot have really good verse without a considerable amount of differentiation between word-accent and verse-ictus, though of course the difference is a matter of art, or perhaps of artifice. In Latin, however, the distinction between word-accent and verse-ictus is of the most fundamental character.

102.   In Latin, as in English, the poet so arranged his words that for the reader they produced rhythm, and in the main he used the pronunciation of daily speech. But metre was determined by relative lengths of syllables, and in the construction of verse everything was subordinated to quantity. Whereas in English a rhythmic effect is, as a rule, brought about by reading a poem according to the accents in standard pronunciation, in Latin the rhythmic effect is brought about by a regular arrangement of long and short syllables. In English we subordinate all questions of quantity to accent. In Latin we subordinate both ictus and even accent to syllable length, though neither ictus nor accent is lost.

It has already been stated that the exact nature of Latin accent is uncertain. In fact the exact nature of accent as we use it in English is uncertain, though it is at least possible, and some authorities think it probable, that in an English word the accented syllable is pitched higher (or lower) than unaccented syllables[1]. If, as some authorities think, the Romans always chanted their verse, and always chanted the accented syllable of a word on a higher note than the unaccented syllables, we can form a pretty clear idea as to the manner in which they brought out both ictus and accent, for in Latin, unlike English, ictus and accent very frequently fell on different syllables.

103. Reference to §§ 91 (1) and 92 (7) will show that the spondee and the dactyl have equivalent time-periods, and it is good practice to read aloud a succession of spondees and dactyls, correctly timed by the metronome. We may take a few lines from Virgil:

> Musa, mihi causas memora, quo numine laeso,
> Quidve dolens, regina deûm tot volvere casus
> Insignem pietate virum, tot adire labores,
> Impulerit. Tantaene animis caelestibus irae?[2]

[1] Cf. Chap. X.

[2] The fundamental mistake made almost universally in the reading of Latin hexameters is, as Mr Mackail happily puts it, to read them as though they were in triple (musical) time, whereas they are, of course, in common time. Once this fact is realised, the rest is comparatively easy.

These may be written to shew the feet, the quantities, and
the accents. Cf. §§ 52 and 73 (The six feet of each verse
are marked off by the longer bars. The short bars indicate
half feet, in order that the time-relations of the spondees
and dactyls may be clearly seen.)

```
Mú- |să mí-|hǐ   |caú- |sās  |mě-mŏ-|rā  |quō |nú- |mǐ-ně|laé-|sǒ
Quíd-|vě dǒ-|lēns |rē-  |gí-  |nă dě-|ún  |tǒt |vǒl-|vě-rě|cá- |sūs
Ín-  |síg-  |něm  |pǐ-ě-|tă-  |tǒ ví-|rǔn |tǒ-tă-|dí-|rě lă-|bǒ-|rēs
Ǐm-  |pú-lě-|rǐt  |Tǎn- |taé- |n'ǎ-nǐ-|mǐs|cae-|les-|tǐ-bǔ-|sí-|rae
```

The ictus falls on the first syllable of each foot. Hence
the ictus and accent coincide in the last two feet of each line,
and also in the case of the words **Mǔsă, quǐdvě, rēgínă,
děǔm**[1], **pǐětátě, Tǎntaéně**. But they do *not* coincide in the
case of **mǐhí, caúsās, mémŏrā, dǒlēns, īnsígněm, vírǔm,
ǐmpúlěrǐt, ánǐmǐs**.

It is not uncommon for members of the older classical
school, when scanning lines like the above, to ignore the
accent altogether unless it happens to coincide with the
ictus. In imitation of sing-song English, they give a heavy
stress to the first syllable of every foot, whether accented
or not, thus subordinating accent to ictus entirely. They
would pronounce **mǐhí** as **mǐhí, caúsās** as **causás, mémŏrā**
as **měmŏrá, īnsígněm** as **ínsīgném, ǐmpúlěrǐt** as **ǐm·
púlěrít**, and so on. This is altogether wrong. It is just as
if, in English, they said *sugár, bázaar, propérty, latítude,
ímportant, ómitting, circúlated, terrítory, ópiníon, éconómy*, &c.
Such a pronunciation would be intolerable, if only because
the ear would often fail to detect the words the speaker used.

There is no justification for scanning in this way. It is
a mere imitation of English accent-rhythm. In Latin it is

---

[1] Authorities disagree about the position of the accent in *deûm* (= *deorum*).

not accent-rhythm, but *quantity-rhythm*, as determined by syllable length, that is the important thing.

104. In reading the lines quoted in the preceding section, it is best to read them first in monotone, with the metronome, both accent and ictus being entirely disregarded: the primary consideration is *time*. The second reading should also be in monotone, but in this case all accented syllables might be pitched in a somewhat higher key,—merely for purposes of differentiation. The ear ought now to be able to detect the natural "swing" of the verse, and the third reading can take place in the ordinary way. When this is done, it is probable that the ictus will make itself felt in every foot, even if we try to suppress it: our English habits make this almost inevitable. Both accent and ictus will thus probably be heard, the accent, however, being the more prominent of the two, and this is exactly what is wanted.—(Cf. § 101.)

105. As in English, *sense-stress* may sometimes fall upon a monosyllable that does not take the ictus, and as in English the ictus may sometimes fall upon a monosyllable that ought not to be stressed at all.—(Cf. § 100; also § 86, II (8), footnote.)

106. The two important things to bear in mind are: (1) Each syllable must be given its proper length, whether accented or not; (2) the heavy ictus heard in English metrical feet must be entirely avoided in Latin. If accurate syllable-length is maintained, and accent is always made as light as possible, the correct reading of Latin poetry ought to cause little difficulty.

107. If, in fact, proper attention be given to accurate syllable-length and to such points as elision, slurring, final *m*, the consonant groups of § 66 (4), &c., Latin poetry may safely be read, as far as regards pronunciation, after the manner of prose. In any case, Latin verse must be pronounced throughout with the prose accent. The poet's systematised metrical arrangement of long and short syllables will then emerge in a quantity-rhythm which ought to be felt as clearly, and appreciated as fully, as accent-rhythm in English.

CHAPTER XIII

WORDS FREQUENTLY MISPRONOUNCED

108. In the following words false quantities are common, no matter whether the restored Roman or the discarded English pronunciation is in use.

(1) ămō, băsĭs, dăbăm, dămŭs, dărĕ, făbă, hăstă, lăbŏr, mănŭs, mēnsă, pătĕr, quădrāgĭntā, quădrŭpēs. (In these words the *ă* is often pronounced as if it were long; in the last two words *quăd-* is very commonly made to rime with *pod* instead of with *păd*[1]. Final short *a* must be pronounced distinctly.—Cf. § 9.)

(2) āc, āctĭō, āctŭm, ămās, ămāns, audĭās, audāx, dāns, ĕrās, frāctŭm, hŏrtāns, ĭllā, māgnŭs, māllĕ, mālŭmŭs, Mārcŭs, māssa, māvīs, māxĭmŭs, mēnsā, mŏnēbās, nārrō, pāctŭm, rādīx, sāl, tāctŭm, vāllŭm, vāstŭs. (In these words the long *a* is often pronounced as if it were short.)

---

[1] Approximately. Cf. §§ 4 (*a*) and 10.

The following groups of words, (3) to (10), are arranged like the above, according to the particular vowel (ĕ, ē, ĭ, ī, ŏ, ō, ŭ, ū), frequently mispronounced, i.e. incorrectly shortened, or incorrectly lengthened.

(3) ămārĕ, bĕnĕ, dĕŭs, dīvĕs, ĕă, ĕīs, ĕnĭm, ĕō, ĕquĕs, ĕŭnt, ĕxpĕdīō, ĭllĕ, ĭpsĕ, lĕō, mĕī, mĕlĭŏr, pŏstĕrĭŏr, sĕnĭŏr, sŭpĕrĭŏr, vĭdĕ[1] (or vĭdē). (Words like ĕă, dĕŭs, lĕō, and mĕī, are difficult to pronounce correctly.—Cf. § 9.)

(4) ămēs, audĭēns, bēstĭă, dēns, ēnsĭs, fēstŭs, gēns, ĭēns, ĭngēns, lēctŭs, lēx, mēns, mēnsă, mētrŏpŏlĭs, mŏnēns, mŏnēs, nōlēns, ŏrchēstră, pēnūrĭă, pĕrēmptŭs, plēbs, pŏtēns, prēndō, prūdēns, quŏtĭēns, rēctŭm, rēgnŭm, rēn, rēx, rēxī, săpĭēns, scēptrŭm, sēcūrŭs, sēgnĭs, tēctŭm, tēxī, tŏtĭēns, vēndō, vērnŭs, vēstīgĭŭm, vŏlēns.

(5) bĭcĕps, dĭēs, fĭdēs, hĭĕmĕ, ĭbĭ, ĭit, ĭtă, māchĭnă, mĭhĭ, mĭnŏr, mĭnŭs, mĭsĕr, nĭhĭl, nĭsĭ, pĭŭs, prĭŏr, quăsĭ, sŏcĭĕtās, trĭbŭs, trĭrēmĭs, ŭbĭ, vĭdĕ (or vĭdē). (In such words as dĭēs, hĭĕmĭ, ĭit, the ĭ requires much practice to pronounce correctly.—Cf. § 9.)

(6) ăntīquŭs, audīs, crīspŭs, dĭē, dīgnŭm, fīlĭŭs, fīrmŭs, fōrtŭītŭs, frīvŏlŭs, īgnōscō, īnsŏlēns, īs (verb), lībērtās, līctŏr, mālīs, māvīs, mīllĕ, mīttō, mŏnērī, nīl, nōbīs, nōnvīs, ŏvīllŭs, prīncĕps, quīn, quīnquĕ, rādīx, rīxă, rŭdīmĕntŭm, sīc, sīs, stīllă, trīstĭs, vēlīs (noun), vēstīgĭŭm, vīllă, vīs.

(7) bŏnŭs, bŏvĭs, cŏmmŏdŭs, dŏmī, dŏmŭm, fŏrcĕps, hĭstŏrĭă, hŏmō, jŏcŭs, mŏdŏ, mŏră, mŏvĕō, nŏtă,

---

[1] vĭdĕ (with short e) is occasionally found (Phaedr., Pers.).

nŏvĕm, pŏlŭs, pŏsĭtĭō, pŏstĕrĭŏr, pŏstĭs, pŏstmŏdŏ, pŏstpōnō, prŏpĭŏr, prōvŏcō, quōmŏdŏ, rŏsă, sŏcĭŭs, vŏlēns, vŏlō, vŏlŭnt.—Cf. § 9.

(8) bōs¹, cŏllăbōrārĕ, cōnfōrmō, cōnscĭĕntĭă, cōnscĭŭs, cōnsŭl, fōns, fōrtŭītŭs, frōns, hōc, lăbōrārĕ, mōnstrō, mōs, nōllĕ, nōlīs, nōmĭnĭs, nōn, nōnnĕ, nōnvīs, nōscō, ōllă, ōrdō, ōrnō, ōstĭŭm, pōns, pōscă, prōmptŭm, prōspĕrō, prōspĕrŭs, rōstrŭm, Sōcrătēs, sōl, sōlĭtūdō, vōx.

(9) cŭmŭlŭs, dŭŏ, hŭmī, pŭgĭl, lŭpŭs, rŭdīmĕntŭm, sŭmŭs, sŭīs, sŭŭs, ŭrbs, vŏlŭmŭs, ĕxŭltō, gŭttă.— Cf. §§ 10, 11.

(10) cūr, frūstrā, frūstŭm, fūstĭs, jūstŭs, jūxtă, lūx, nūllŭs, nūntĭŭs, nūntĭō, plūs, rūs, rūstĭcŭs, strūctŭm, sūmptŭm, ūltĭmŭs.

109. Incorrect accent. In the following and many other words, the accent is often placed on the antepenult instead of on the penult:

mĭnístĕr, măgístĕr, hŏnéstās, hărúspĕx, prŏfícĭscŏr, lībér-tās, sŭpérstĕs, paupértās, săcérdōs, Lŭpércăl, tăbérnă, făcúltās, sĭmúltās, vŏlúntās, vŏlúptās, săgíttă, sătéllĕs, sŭpéllĕx, dĭscĭplínă, ĭnŏdórŭs, fōrtŭítŭs, &c., &c.

In the following words the accent is often placed on the penult instead of on the antepenult:

máchĭnă, sóbrĭŭs, prístĭnŭs, cómmŏdŭs, vŏlŭmŭs, pró-vŏcō, quómŏdŏ, pŏstmŏdŏ, pŏtŭérĭm, nĭhĭlómĭnŭs, &c., &c.

110. Latin words are frequently mispronounced because of their resemblance to English words. Cf. Lat.

---

¹ It is a curious fact that *bōs*, *bŏvĭs*, is very often pronounced *bŏs*, *bōvĭs*.

sŭpĕrĭŏr and Eng. *superior*; āctĭō and *action*; scēptrŭm with *sceptre*; vēstīgĭŭm and *vestige*; mĭsĕr and *miser*; sŏcĭĕtās, *society*; ŏlívă, *olive*; crīspŭs, *crisp*; frīvŏlŭs, *frivolous*; īnsŏlēns, *insolent*; lībĕrtās, *liberty*; cŏmmŏdŭs, *commodious*; nŏvĕm, *November*; pŏstpōnō, *postpone*; cōnscĭŭs, *conscious*; nōmĭnĭs, *nominal*; prōspĕrō, *prosperous*; sōlĭtūdō, *solitude*; jūstŭs, *just*; rūstĭcŭs, *rusticate*; mĭnĭstĕr, *minister*; măgĭstĕr, *magistrate*; hŏnĕstās, *honesty*; făcŭltas, *faculty*; ĭnŏdŏrŭs, *inodorous*; máchĭna, *machine*; ĕxcéllēns = eks-kél-lēnss, *excellent*; ămbĭtĭō, *ambition*; and a large number of others[1]. The known pronunciation of the corresponding English word (not necessarily corresponding in meaning) seems to act as a trap for the unwary.

111. The following are a few examples of false quantities heard, during the last two or three years, in the House of Commons, the Law Courts, the pulpit, the public platform, and elsewhere. The Latin phrase, correctly marked, appears on the left; the words as incorrectly pronounced on the right:

(1)	cētĕrīs părĭbŭs	cĕtĕrĭs.
(2)	cui bŏnō?	bōnō.
(3)	prō bŏnō pūblĭcō	bōnō, pŭblĭcō.
(4)	dē mŏrtŭĭs, nīl nĭsĭ bŏnŭm	mŏrtŭĭs, nĭl, nĭsī, bŏnŭm.
(5)	cĭrcŭlŭs in prŏbăndō	prŏbăndō.
(6)	cŭm grānō sălĭs	sălĭs.
(7)	făcĭlĕ prīncĕps	făcĭlē, prīncĕps.
(8)	prīncĭpĭă nōn hŏmĭnēs	prīncĭpĭă, nŏn.
(9)	fĭdĕĭ dēfēnsŏr	fĭdĕĭ, dēfēnsŏr.
(10)	bŏnā fĭdē	bōnă, fĭdĕ.
(11)	mălā fĭdē	mālă, fĭdĕ.

[1] It may be observed that the ordinary everyday blunders made by *pupils* are not included in §§ 108—110.

(12) fōns ĕt ŏrīgō	fŏns, ōrīgō.
(13) ŏrīgō mălī	ōrīgō, mălī.
(14) fŏrtĭtĕr ĕt rēctă	fŏrtĭtĕr, rĕctă.
(15) in lŏcō părĕntĭs	lŏcō.
(16) in mĕdĭās rēs	mēdĭās.
(17) vĭă mĕdĭă	vĭă, mĕdĭă.
(18) in mĕmŏrĭăm	mĕmōrĭăm.
(19) in sĭtū	sĭtū.
(20) lăbŏr ŏmnĭă vĭncĭt	lăbŏr.
(21) lēx nōn scrīptă	lĕx, nŏn, scrīptă.
(22) lŏcŭs in quō	lŏcŭs.
(23) lŏcŭm tĕnēns	lŏcŭm, tĕnĕns.
(24) măgnŭm ŏpŭs	măgnŭm, ōpŭs.
(25) mēns sānă in cŏrpŏrĕ sānō	mĕns.
(26) mŏdŭs ŏpĕrăndī	mōdŭs.
(27) nĕcĕssĭtās nōn hăbĕt lēgĕm	nŏn, lĕgĕm.
(28) nĕ plūs ūltrā	plŭs, ŭltră.
(29) nĭl dēspērăndŭm	nĭl, dĕspĕrăndŭm.
(30) nōlēns vŏlēns	nōlĕns, vōlĕns.
(31) nōn sĕquĭtŭr	nŏn.
(32) nŏtă bĕnĕ	nōtă, bĕnĕ.
(33) ŏdĭŭm thĕŏlŏgĭcŭm	ōdĭŭm, thĕŏlŏgĭcŭm.
(34) pĕtītĭō prīncĭpĭī	pĕtĭtĭō, prīncĭpĭī.
(35) poētă născĭtŭr, nōn fĭt	născĭtŭr, nŏn.
(36) rĕquĭēscăt in pācĕ	rĕquĭĕscăt, păcĕ.
(37) sĭnĕ dĭē	sīnĕ, dĭĕ.
(38) sĭnĕ quā nōn	sīnĕ, nŏn.
(39) sī vīs pācĕm, părā bĕllŭm	vīs, păcĕm, pāră.
(40) stătū quō ăntĕ bĕllŭm	stătū.
(41) suăvĭtĕr in mŏdō, fŏrtĭtĕr in rē	suāvítĕr, mōdō, fŏrtĭtĕr.
(42) sŭb rŏsă	rōsă.
(43) sŭī gĕnĕrĭs	sŭī.
(44) tū quŏquĕ	quŏquĕ.
(45) ŭltĭmă rătĭō rēgŭm	rătĭō, rĕgŭm.
(46) vēlīs et rēmīs	vēlĭs, rēmĭs.
(47) in vīnō vērĭtās	vĕrĭtās.
(48) vōx pŏpŭlī	vŏx.

These false quantities are more commonly heard in the "old" (the "English") pronunciation than in the Roman. Greater accuracy almost invariably follows the adoption of the Roman pronunciation, presumably because the mere act of making the change necessitates greater attention being given to quantity.

112. Roby gives a useful list of words (*Grammar*, Vol. I, p. XC) with the approximately correct phonetic English spelling. But they are only approximations after all, and it is best not to imitate them. It is, in fact, almost impossible to represent a word like *fĭĕrī* in phonetic English, unless phonetic symbols are used[1].

Professor Postgate also gives a very helpful list of words, with imitated pronunciation.—See p. 118 of his *New Latin Primer*. By means of the use of different type, he contrives to give, in numerous phrases, English phonetic equivalents almost identical with the originals. To those engaged in teaching the examples are very suggestive.

CHAPTER XIV

EXERCISES

It is of little avail merely to read through a chapter dealing with new or unusual sounds. Accuracy can be acquired only by considerable practice, and the reader is urged to select a few words illustrating each particular sound (vowel and consonant) and to pronounce them aloud several times in succession. The following short lists will probably suffice for the purpose:

[1] Cf. the artifice suggested at the end of § 9.

The vowels.—Read §§ 1—11.

a: făbă, dătă, ărmă, cástră, clāră, pācăt, strātă, plāgā, ārās, frăgrāns, ămās, ălăpă, ămābăt, clāmābăt.

e: těněr, sěmpěr, pěctěn, ěssě, něcně, běně, ēssě, sēdēs, tēctē, pědēs, běllē, pětěrě, pěrděrě, rěpěntē, pěndērě, dēběrě, dēlērēs.

i: tǐgrǐs, bǐbǐt, sǐbǐ, mǐhǐ, pīlī, prīmī, pǐrī, sǐbī, crīnǐs, trīstǐs, sǐmǐlǐs, ǐmprǐmǐs, ǐmprīmīs, mīlǐtǐs, mǐnǐstrī, dǐscrīmǐnǐs.

o: mŏdŏ, mŏdō, sŏrŏr, ŏdŏr, cōgō, ōrdō, mōnstrō, nōscō, cōnsŏrs, tōnsŏr, uŏmō, uŏluō, bŏnō, cōgnōscō, cŏndōnō, rōbŏrō, cŏŏptō.

u: sŭmŭs, lŭpŭs, sŭŭs, ŭrsŭs, bŭlbŭs, fŭrfŭr, ūsūs, frūctūs, frūctŭs, fūmŭs, mūnŭs, mūscŭs, būbŭlŭs, cŭmŭlŭs, mūscŭlŭs.

y: gȳrŭs, Tȳrŭs, ŏnȳx, mȳrtŭs, lȳră, crȳptă, păpȳrŭs, Sȳrǐă, Bȳzăntǐŭm, Pȳrrhŭs, Măssȳlī, pȳrămǐs, gōrȳ-tŭs, Hȳlās.

The common diphthongs.—Read §§ 12—16.

ae: aedēs, aestās, caecŭs, caedēs, Paeān, mǐnae, mēnsae, taedae, aestǐmō, praebērě, paedăgōgŭs, taenǐae, Aetnă, saepǐssǐmē.

au: audǐō, aulă, aură, augŭr, auctŭs, austērŭs, caudă, fraus, gauděō, laudō, laus, paupěr, raucŭs, taurŭs.

oe: poenă, ămoenŭs, cōmoedǐă, foedārě, moenǐă, oecŏ-nŏmǐă, Oedǐpūs, Oenōtrŭs.

Consonantal i (j) = y.—Read §§ 54—61.

Iānŭs (Jānŭs), ǐăcěō (jăcěō), ǐānŭārǐŭs ⁊(jānŭārǐŭs), ǐēcī (jēcī), ǐěcŭr (jěcŭr), dēǐěctŭs (dējěctŭs), ēǐēcī (ējēcī), ǐŏcŭs (jŏcŭs), ǐŭbă (jŭbă), ǐūs (jūs), māǐŏr (mājŏr), pēǐŏr (pējŏr), māǐěstās (mājěstās).

Consonantal u (v) = **w**.

brĕuĭs (brĕvĭs), făuŏr (făvŏr), pāuō (pāvō), sprēuī
(sprēvī), prīuŭs (prīvŭs), sĕruŭs (sĕrvŭs), uăccă
(văccă), uāstŭs (vāstŭs), uĕllĕ (vĕllĕ), uĭă (vĭă), uŏlō
(vŏlō), uŭlnŭs (vŭlnŭs), uĭx (vĭx), uōx (vōx).

Consonants.

c :—Read § 23.—ācĕr, ăcĕr, cēră, cĕcĭdī, cĕcīdī, cĕcĭnī, cĭbŭs,
cĭcĕr, ŏcĕĭdō, ŏccīdō, făcētŭs, pĭscīnă, spĕcĭēs, sŏcĭĕtās,
crŭcĭārĕ.

ch.—Read § 24.—chărtă, chĭmaeră, chălўbs, chŏlĕră, līchēn,
māchĭnă, schēmă, pŭlchĕr, Ăchĕrōn, chăŏs.

g.—Read § 27.—gĕnĕr, gēns, lĕgĕrĕ, pĭgĕr, prōgĕnĭēs, sĕgĕs,
ăgĭtō, ĭgĭtŭr, măgĭstĕr, gĕnĭŭs, gĕnŭs, dĭgĭtŭs, pāgĭnă.

nc.—Read § 35.—ăncĕps, căncĕr, cīnctŭs, răncŏr, prīncĕps,
plānctŭs, cŏncĭpĕrĕ, cŏncŏrdĭă, ĭncīdō, trŭncŭs, quīncūnx.

ng.—Read §§ 37—38.—fŭngī, lŏngŭs, ăngĭnă[1], ăngūstŭs,
cŏngrŭĕrĕ, ŭngŭlă, frăngĕrĕ, cŏnjŭngerĕ ; ănguĭs,
sănguĭs, pĭnguĭs, ŭnguĭs, lĭnguă, lănguŏr.

ph.—Read § 42.—phălănx, phăntăsmă, prŏphētă, phrĕnēsĭs,
sphĭnx, grăphĭŭm, lўmphă, mĕtămŏrphōsĭs, nўmphă,
sўmphōnĭă, sīphō.

r.—Read § 44.—Rōmă, rārē, cŏrōnă, ărmă, ărbĭtĕr, mŏrŏr,
cărcĕr, hŏrrŏr, ĕrrŏr, tĕrrŏr, mărmŏr, sŭrdŭs, rōrārĭī,
frŭŏr, ămŏr.   (This is a difficult exercise.)

s.—Read § 46.—băsĭlĭcă, ōtĭōsŭs, pausă, pŏsĭtĭō, praesēns,
rĕgēns, părs, rēs, ŭrbs, trăbs, uŭlpēs, sŏbŏlēs, trāns,

---

[1] Stowasser, Heinichen, Feyerabend, and others give ăngĭnă, but this
is wrong.

pōns, dēns. (Avoid the tendency to convert the s, especially s final, into a z.) Scīpĭō, scĭĕntĭă, scītē, scĭlĭcĕt, scēptrŭm.

t.—Read § 48.—āctĭō, lātĭō, lēctĭō, nŏtātĭō, rătĭō, ămīcĭtĭă, ămbĭtĭō, cĭtĭŭs, cŏmĭtĭă, grātĭă, laetĭtĭă, sĕntĕntĭă, tŏlĕrăntĭă.

th.—Read § 49.—thălămŭs, thĕātrŭm, thrŏnŭs, căthĕdră, āthlētă, aethēr, ēthĭcă, spăthŭlă, măthēmătĭcă, thōrāx, cĭthără.

x.—Read § 50.—pāx, rēx, lēx, ĕxīlĭs, ĕxpĕdĭō, ĕxĕrcĭtŭs, ĕxcĕlsŭs, ĕxŭltō, ĕxĭtĭŭm, ĕxĭgŭŭs, ĕxāmĕn, ĕxăspĕrō, ĕxāctĭō, tĕxtĭlĭs. (Avoid converting the x = ks into the sound of gz; ĕxīlĭs = ĕk-sī-lĭs, not ĕg-zī-lĭs. Note also that ĕxcĕlsŭs = ĕks-kĕl-sŭs: ĕxcĕllēns = ĕks-kĕl-lēnss.)

Double consonants.—Read §§ 62–3.

ăccĭdĕrĕ, ăccĭpĕrĕ, flăccĭdŭs, flŏccŭs, săccŭs; ăddō, ăddūcō, rĕddō, rĕddĭtŭs, ăddĭctĭō; ĕffĕctŭs, dĭffīdĭt, ŏffĕndō, ĕffŏdĭō, ŏffĭcĭŭm; ăggrĕgō, ĕxăggĕrō, ăggĕr, sŭggĕrō; ăllūdō, bĕllŭm, căllĭs, prŏcĕllă, căpĭllŭs; sŭmmŭm, cŏmmŏdŭm, cŏmmūnĕm, cŏmmōtŭm, ĭmmōbĭlĕm; ănnŭlŭs, ănnālĭs, cănnăbĭs, ĭnnŏcēns; ăppĕllō, păppŭs, ŏppĭdŭm, ăppĕtītŭs, ăpplĭcō; ĕrrŏr, cărrŭs, sĕrră, tĕrrĕstrĭs, hŏrrŏr; māssă, ēssĕ, ĕssĕ, tŭssĭs, tĕssĕră; săgĭttă, gŭttă, ăttrītŭs, gŭttŭr, mĭttĭt.

The following pairs of words, though spelt the same, have different quantities, and are therefore pronounced differently. In many cases the meanings are entirely different. In many cases, too, the words are of entirely different etymological origin.

ācĕr	ăcĕr	fūgĭt	fūgĭt	pĕndḗrĕ	pĕndĕrĕ
ămārē	ămārĕ	ĭmprímĭs	ĭmprĭmĭs	pílă	pílă
ămbĭtŭs	ămbĭtŭs	lăbŏr	lăbŏr	plăgă	plăgă
audiḗrĭs	audiĕris	lātē	lātē	pŏpŭlŭs	pŏpŭlŭs
aúdĭt	audít	léctŭs	lĕctŭs	pŏrrígō	pŏrrígō
cānĭs	cănĭs	lēgĕrĕ	lĕgĕrĕ	pótĭō	pótĭō
cĕcídĭ	cĕcĭdĭ	lévĭs	lĕvĭs	praedícō	praédícō
cŏncídō	cŏncĭdō	líbĕr	líbĕr	prĭstínŭs	prístĭnŭs
cŏncĭtŭs	cŏncĭtŭs	líbĕt	líbĕt	quŏquĕ	quŏquĕ
cŏndĭtŭs	cŏndĭtŭs	lūstrŭm	lūstrŭm	rātīs	rătĭs
cōnsĭdĕrĕ	cōnsídĕrĕ	mălŭm	mălŭm	rĕlégō	rĕlĕgō
cŏnvíctŭs	cŏnvíctŭs	mānēs	mănēs	rŏsă	rŏsă
cŭpídō	cŭpĭdō	mĭsérĕ	mĭsĕrĕ	sālīs	sălĭs
dícō	dícō	mŏlĭs	mŏlĭs	sérŭm	sérŭm
ēdō	ĕdō	nítŏr	nítŏr	sōlŭm	sōlŭm
ĕdúcăt	ĕdŭcăt	nŏstrās	nŏstrās	sŭccídĕrĕ	sŭccídĕrĕ
ēs	ĕs	ŏccídĕrĕ	ŏccídĕrĕ	sŭspícĭō	sŭspícĭō
ēssĕ	ēssĕ	ōs	ŏs	útī	útī
ēst	ĕst	păctŭs	păctŭs	vādō	vădō
fídĭt	fídĭt	pălŭs	pălūs	vénĭt	vénĭt
frētŭs	frĕtus	pārĕrĕ	părĕrĕ	vĕstrās	vĕstrās
fríctŭs	fríctŭs	pārēns	părēns	víctŭm	vĭctŭm

In regard to those words with an accent on the last syllable, see § 86 II (2).

The following groups of words are intended for practice in the different types detailed in §§ 92, 93. In order to obtain the correct relative lengths of the syllables in the words of each type, the English words suggested in §§ 92, 93 should first be uttered, deliberately and distinctly. Special attention should be paid to the position of the accent.

§ 92 (1) nōlítō, lēgátōs, nōlébās, cālígō, rādícēs, fīébās, iūráuī, ĕxpăndŭnt, cŏmpíngō, cōmpléuī, cŏllídĕnt, rēxérunt, ĕxcéllēns, ămpléctī.

7—2

§ 92 (2) rĕpónō, sălútō, ămátī, ămábās, ĭmágō, ămícae, pĕrsónae, ĕquéstrī, sŭpĕrbō, mŏnébănt, rŭíssĕnt, făcŭltās, săcĕrdōs.

§ 92 (3) nātúră, lōrícă, lēgálĕ, fīébăm, pācátă, audímŭr, praecaútŭs, frōndósă, fōrmícă, ŏctāuŭs, cŏmpĕrtŭm, sĕrpĕntĭs, quōrŭndăm.

§ 92 (4) cŏrónă, ămárĕ, ămátă, pŭdórĭs, ămábăr, uĭdétŭr, clŏácă, sĕpŭltŭm, Dĕcĕmbĕr, fŭíssĕt, tăbĕlla, sĕcúrĭs, bĕátă.

§ 92 (5) cíuĭtās, fílĭōs, lítĭgō, dílĭgō, díuĭdō, aúdĭēs, próuŏcō, cénsŭī, réxĕrās, máxĭmē, próspĕrō, scălpsĕrĭnt, cŏmprĭmō.

§ 92 (6) lăpĭdēs, mŏnĕō, mŏuĕō, părĭēs, cŭmŭlō, nŭmĕrō, ădămās, cécĭnī, uŏlŭcrēs, căpĭĕnt, sălĭŭnt, mŏnŭī, fŭĕrĭnt.

§ 92 (7) árĕă, líbĕră, línĕă, pónĕrĕ, quómŏdŏ, naútĭcă, aúlĭcă, bárbără, ímprŏbă, sŭbdĭtŭm, pŏssŭmŭs, máchĭnă, béstĭă.

§ 92 (8) fácĕrĕ, mŏnĕŏr, régĕrĕ, ănĭmă, érĭmŭs, fíĕrĕm, férŭlă, mŏnŭĭt, régĭmŭs, ăpĭcĭs, mŏnĭtŭs, lácrĭma, uŏlŭmŭs, régĭtĭs.

§ 93 (1) ōrātórēs, īnfēlícēs, uēnātórēs, ēmĕndáuī, dēlēuérŭnt, cŏmpēgíssĕnt, ĕxpĕrgíscī, dīctātórēs, nōnāgíntā.

§ 93 (2) rĕcūsáuī, rĕtărdáuī, sălūtáuī, ăgāsónēs, ŏblīuíscī, cĕcīdérŭnt, cŭcŭrrérŭnt, cĕcīdíssĕnt, quădrāgíntā.

§ 93 (3) ēlăbórō, glōrĭósē, mágnĭtúdō, cōnfĭtérī, ăltĭtúdō, ŏppĕrírī, lăssĭtúdō, mīscŭérŭnt, audĭébās.

§ 93 (4) uĕnĕrárī, prŏfĭcíscī, tĕnŭíssĕnt, Mĭtўlénē, dŏcŭérŭnt, rĕsĕráuī, spĕcŭlárī, ĭmĭtárī, mŏnŭíssĕnt.

§ 93 (5) nōlītŏtĕ, ōrātŏrĭs, ăccūsătŭs, rĕspŏndĕrĕ, hŏrtā-
bámŭr, cŏmmūtárĕ, rēxĭssémŭs, hŏrtābŭntŭr,
hŏrtārémŭr.

§ 93 (6) cŏrōnárĕ, cŏlōrárĕ, uĭătŏrĭs, ămāuĭstĭs, ămābámŭr,
ămārémŭs, rŭdīméntŭm, Lŭpĕrcálĭs, Dŏlābéllă.

§ 93 (7) lītĭgátŏr, rēxĕrátĭs, augŭrárĕ, ēmĭgrárĕ, īnsŏlén-
tĕm, ănnŭálĕ, audĭámŭr, audĭéntŭr, ăggrĕgárĕ.

§ 93 (8) ănĭmárĕ, fūrĭósŭs, mŏnŭĭstĭs, uŏlŭĭssĕm, ĕpĭ-
grămmă, nŭmĕrárĕ, sŏcĭárĕ, hŏmĭcídă, căpĭtálĕ.

§ 93 (9) hērédĭtās, frūgálĭtās, pōtátĭō, audímĭnī, fŏrtĭssĭmī,
sēcéssĭō, pŏstrídĭē, mŏllĭssĭmae, ĭndŭlgēō.

§ 93 (10) sĕuérĭtās, rŏgátĭō, rĕbéllĭō, ămáuĕrănt, mŏnémĭnī,
ămáuĕrĭnt, ămámĭnī, prŏbátĭō, rĕmĭscēō.

§ 93 (11) fūtĭlĭtās, mālŭĕrō, ēgrégĭē, bēstĭŏlae, rēlĭgĭō, ăc-
cŭmŭlō, Pausánĭās, lūxŭrĭēs, tĕrrĭfícănt.

§ 94 (12) cĕlérĭtās, mŏnŭĕrō, sŏcĭĕtās, mĭsĕrĭae, mŏnŭĕrās,
mŏnŭĕrīs, rĕcŭpĕrō, căpímĭnī, rĕmóuĕō.

§ 94 (13) mirábĭlĕ, tībícĭnă, dēlúdĕrĕ, fānátĭcă, īnsánĭă,
cōgnóscĕrĕ, dĭscŏrdĭă, ĕmpírĭcŭs, ĭntérprĕtĭs.

§ 94 (14) pĕcúnĭă, cŏlónĭă, dŏméstĭcă, pŏténtĭă, căpéssĕrĕ,
bŏárĭă, ĭnútĭlĕ, ămábĕrĭs, ămáuĕrăm.

§ 94 (15) mātérĭă, mīrífĭcă, mālŭĕrăm, ăttŏnĭtă, ŏpprímĕrĕ,
cŏrpŏrĕă, grămmátĭcă, ĭmprímĕrĕ, ŏbstrĕpĭtŭm.

§ 94 (16) mĕmŏrĭă, cănŏnĭcă, băsílĭcă, părábŏlă, mŭlíĕrĭs,
rĕfícĕrĕ, pŏtŭĕrăm, quădrŭpĕdĕ, săcrílĕgă.

CHAPTER XV

1. In the following passage from Caesar, the marking is in accordance with the principles laid down in the standard work of Dr Bos. The marking is modified to suit English readers:

Gallia est omnis divisa in partes tres, quarum unam incolunt Belgae, aliam Aquitani, tertiam, qui ipsorum lingua Celtae, nostra Galli appellantur. Hi omnes lingua, institutis, legibus inter se differunt. Gallos ab Aquitanis Garumna flumen, a Belgis Matrona et Sequana dividit. Horum omnium fortissimi sunt Belgae, propterea quod a cultu atque humanitate provinciae longissime absunt, minimeque ad eos mercatores saepe commeant, atque ea, quae ad effeminandos animos pertinent, important, proximique sunt Germanis

Gắl-lĭᵃ ĕs tŏm-nĭs dĭ-wĭ-sᵃ ĭn-pắr-tēs trēs, kwắrᵘ únⁱ ĭn-cŏ-lŭnt Bĕl-gae, ắ-lĭᵃ A-kwĭ-tắ-nī, tĕr-tĭ-ắᵐ, kwⁱĭp-sŏ-rŭl-lĭn-gwā Kĕl-tae, nŏs-trā Gắl-lⁱ ắp-pĕl-lắn-tŭr. Hⁱŏm-nēs lĭn-gwā, īn-stĭ-tú-tīs, lĕ-gĭ-bŭ sĭn-tĕr sē dĭf-fĕ-rŭnt. Gắl-lō sắ-bă-kwī-tắ-nīs Ga-rŭm-nă flú-mĕn, ā-bĕl-gīs Mắ-trŏ-nᵃ ĕt-Sĕ-kwă-nă dĭ-wĭ-dĭt. Hŏ-rᵘŏm-nĭ-ŭn-fŏr-tĭs-sĭ-mī sŭnt Bĕl-gae, prŏp-tĕ-rĕ-ā kwŏ dā-kŭl-tᵘắt-kwᵉ hū-mā-nĭ-tắ-tĕ prō-vĭn-cĭ-ae lŏn-gĭs-sĭ-mᵉắb-sŭnt, mĭ-nĭ-mĕ-kwᵉắ-dĕ-ōs mĕr-cā-tŏ-rēs saé-pĕ cŏm-mĕ-ănt, ắt-kwᵉĕ-ă, kwᵃᵉắ-dĕf-fĕ-mĭ-nắn-dō sắ-nĭ-mōs pĕr-tĭ-nĕnt, ĭm-pŏr-tănt, prŏk-sĭ-mĭ-kwĕ sŭnt Gĕr-mắ-nīs

qui trans Rhenum incolunt,
quibuscum   continenter
bellum gerunt.

kwī trāns Rhé-n^{a}ín-cŏ-lŭnt,
kwĭ-bŭs-cung cŏn-tĭ-nĕn-tĕr
bĕl-lung gĕ-rŭnt.

2. The following passage, from Cicero's *Orator*, is shown as marked by Ellis. Ellis assumes that his ordinary rules for pronunciation are known, and here he draws attention merely to the two points most frequently forgotten, viz., syllable length, and the treatment of *m* final[1]. (Very slightly modified):

In versu quidem theatra tota exclamant, si fuit una syllaba brevior aut longior. Nec vero multitudo pedes novit, nec ullos numeros tenet; nec illud, quod offendit, aut cur, aut in quo offendat, intelligit; et tamen omnium longitudinum et brevitatum in sonis, sicut acutarum graviumque vocum, judicium ipsa natura in auribus nostris collocavit.

In- ver-sū quiden- theātra tōta ex-clāman-t sī fuit ūnā syl-labā brevior aut lon-gior. Nec vērō mul-titūdō pedēs-nōvit, nec ul-lōs- numerōs-tenet; nec il-lud-, quod of-fen-dit, aut cūr, aut in- quō of-fen-dat, in-tel-ligit; et- ta-men om-niul- lon-gitūdinu^{m} et- brevitātu^{m} īn-sonīs, sīcut acūtārung- graviúm-que vō-cun- jūdiciu^{m} ip-sa nātūra in auribus- nostrīs col-locāvit.

3. The following passage from the *Aeneid* is shown (1) as ordinarily printed; (2) as marked by Dr Bos (slightly modified); (3) as marked by Ellis (slightly modified); and (4) "barred" in order to indicate graphically the relative length of the syllables.

[1] Ellis places a hyphen after a consonant that "makes position." But the hyphen after *ta-* (8th line) and after *vō-* (11th line) is due to exigencies of printing, and merely indicate division of words between two lines.

(1)

Conticuere omnes, intentique ora tenebant;
Inde toro pater Aeneas sic orsus ab alto:
　Infandum, Regina, jubes renovare dolorem;
Trojanas ut opes et lamentabile regnum
Eruerint Danai: quaeque ipse miserrima vidi,
Et quorum pars magna fui. Quis, talia fando,
Myrmidonum, Dolopumve, aut duri miles Ulixi,
Temperet a lacrimis? et jam nox humida caelo
Praecipitat, suadentque cadentia sidera somnos.

(2)

Kŏn-tĭkŭér͞ĕ ŏm-nēs, ĭn-tĕn-tíkw͞ĕ ŏ́ră̆ tĕnébănt;
Ín-dĕ tŏ́rō pắtĕ rae-néās sī-kŏ́r-sŭ să̆ bă̆l-tō:
Īn-fắn-dŭr, rēgínă̆, yŭbēs rĕnŏwắrĕ dŏlŏ́rem;
Trōyánā sŭ-tŏ́pē sĕt-lāmĕn-tábĭlĕ rég-nŭm
Erŭ̆ĕrĭnt Dắnă̆ī: kwaekw͞ĕíp-sĕ mĭsér-rĭmă̆ wídī,
Et-kwŏ́rŭm pars mắg-nă̆ fŭ̆ī. Kwĭs-tá̆-lĭ̆-ă̆ fắn-dō,
Mȳr-mídŏnŭn, Dŏlŏpŭ̆mw͞ĕ, aut-dúrī mílĕ sŭ̆-lŷs-sei,
Tĕ́m-pĕrĕ tā-lá̆-krĭmī sĕt-yă̆n-nŏk súmĭdă̆ kaélō
Prae-kípĭtă̆t, swādént-kwe kă̆dén-tĭ̆ă̆ sídĕră̆ sŏ́m-nŏs.

(3)

Con-ticuére óm-nēs, in-ten-tíque o͝ra tenéban-t;
Ín-de tórō páter Aenéās- sīc ór-sus ab ál-tō:
Īn-fán-dur-, rēgína, júbēs- renováre dolóren-;
Trōjánās ut ópēs et- lāmen-tábile rég-num
Ērúerin-t Dánaī: quaeque íp-se misér-rima ví-dī,
Et- quórum- pár-s mág-na fúī. Quís- tá̆lia fán-dō,
Myr-mídonun- Dolopún-ve aut- dúrī mīles Ulíx-ī,
Tém-peret ā lácrymīs? et- ján- nóx- húmida coélō
Praecípitat-, svādén-tque cadén-tia sídera sóm-nōs-.

(4)

♩ or ♪		♩ or ♪		♩ or ♪		♩ or ♪		♪		♩	
Cŏn-	tĭ-cŭ-	ē-	r'ŏm-	nēs	In-	tĕn-	tí-	quᵉŏ-	rä tĕ-	nĕ-	bänt
Ĭn-	dĕ tŏ-	rō	pä-tĕ-	rae-	nē-	ās	sí-	cōr-	sŭ-să-	băl-	tŏ
Īn-	fān-	dŭm	rē-	gĭ-	nă jŭ-	bēs	rĕ-nŏ-	vä-	rĕ dŏ-	lŏ-	rĕm
Trō-	jā-	nä-	sŭ-tŏ-	pē-	sĕt	lā-	mĕn-	tä-	bĭ-lĕ	rēg-	nŭm
Ē-	rŭ-ĕ-	rĭnt	dă-nă-	ī	quae-	quᵉ ip-	sĕ mĭ-	sĕr	rí-mă	ví-	dī
Et	quŏ-	rŭm	pärs	māg-	nă fŭ-	ī	quís	tä-	lĭ-ă	făn-	dŏ
Mўr-	mĭ-dŏ-	nŭn	dŏ-lŏ-	pŭn-	vᵉaut	dū-	rí	mĭ-	lĕ-sŭ-	lўs-	sei
Tĕm-	pĕ-rĕ-	tä	lă-crĭ-	mĭ-	sĕt	jăn	nŏx	hŭ-	mĭ-dă-	cae-	lŏ
Prae-	cĭ-pĭ-	tăt	suä-	dent-	quĕ că-	dĕn-	tĭ-ă	sí-	dĕ-rä	sŏm-	nŏs

4. Sécheresse indicates the first syllable of each metrical foot by printing the contained vowel in Clarendon type. The artifice is useful:

Lăócoōn dúctus Neptŭnō sórte sacérdōs
Sollémnēs taúrum ĭngéntem mactắbat ad ắrās.
Ecce aútem géminī ā Ténedo tranquílla per álta
(Horréscō réferēns) imménsīs órbibus ángués
Incúmbunt pélagō paritérque ad lítora téndunt;
Péctora quórum inter flúctūs arrécta jubaéque
Sanguíneae exsúperant úndās, pars cétera póntum
Póne légit sinuántque imménsa volúmine térga.

5. In his book *How to pronounce Latin*, Professor Postgate transcribes some passages of Ancient Latin into a phonetic script based upon the system of the *Association Phonétique Internationale*. Two of these passages are here reproduced. It should be noticed that

(1)   The vowel values are in accordance with the symbols given in the last column of the tabulated scheme on page 8.

(2)   ã, ẽ, &c., mean that the word is nasalised.

(3)   Consonantal *i* (*i̯*) is represented by j.

(4)   Consonantal *u* (*u̯*) is represented by w.

(5)   *c* (*q*) is represented by k.

(6)   *n* before *c* (*q*) or *g* is represented by ŋ.

(7)   Trilled *r* is represented by *r*.

(8)   Breathed *r* is represented by *rh*.

(9)   The sign ⊢ represents the vowel sound referred to in § 8 (page 6)[1].

---

[1] This sign is found on extant inscriptions. (See *How to Pronounce Latin*, p. 28.) According to Quintilian, the sign was invented by the Emperor Claudius for the purpose of expressing this particular sound.

(10) Final vowels slurred on to initial vowels are printed
      above the line. So also nasalised vowels. Thus
      omniᵃ, kaus·sa:rᵘ.

(11) The division of syllables is marked where necessary
      by a full stop : kɔl·ligo:, had·ria:tiki:.

(12) A - shows that the two words are pronounced as
      one : ìn-manìbùs.

I. Septimus mihi līber orīginum est in manibus:
    sept⊦mùs mìhi líb:er ɔrí:gìnũst ìn-manìbùs

omnia antīquitātis monumenta colligō: caussārum inlū-
ɔmuìᵃ antí:kwìta:tìs mɔn⊦menta cɔl·lìgo: kaus·sa:rᵘ inlú:-

strium quāscumque dēfendī nunc cum māximē cōnficiō
strìum kwa:skùɒkwɛ de:fendí: nùɒk kùm-ma:ks⊦me: cɔ:nflcìˀ

ōrātiōnēs; iūs augurium pontificium cīɥīle tractō:
o:ra:tìo:ne:s; jú:s aùgùrìùm pɔntìfìkìùm kí:wí:lɛ trakto:

multum etiam Graecīs litterīs útor, Pȳthagorēōrumque
mùltᵘ etìam graekí:s lí:t·terí:s ú:tɔr, py:thagɔre:o:rùɒkwɛ

mōre exercendae memoriae grātiā quid quōque diē
mo:rᵉ ekserkɛndae memɔrìae gra:tìa: kwìd kwo:kwɛ dìe:

dīxerim audierim commemorō ɥesperī.
dí:kserⁱ audìerìm cɔm·memɔro: wesperí:

                              From CICERO de Senectute.

II.   Phasēlus ille quem ɥidētis hospitēs
      phase:lus il·lɛ kwɛm w⊦de:tis hɔspite:s

      ait fuisse nāɥium celerrimus
      ait fuis·sɛ na:wium kelɛr·rimus

      neque ūllius natantis impetum trabis
      nɛkwᵉ u:l·lius natantis impɛtum trabis

nequīsse   praeterīre   sīụe   palmulīs
nɛkwiːs·sɛ   praɛteriːrɛ   siːwɛ   palmuliːs

opus foret ụolāre sīụe linteō
ɔpus fɔrɛt wɔlaːrɛ siːwɛ linteō

et hōc negat minācis Hadriāticī
ɛt hoːk nɛgat minaːkis had·ria:tikī

negāre lītus īnsulāsụe Cycladas
nɛgaːrɛ liːtus iːnsulaːswɛ kyk·ladas

Rhodumque nōbilem horridamque Thrāciam
rhɔduɒkwɛ   noːbilᵉ   hɔr·ridaɒkwɛ thraːkiam

Propontida trucemụe Ponticum sinum.
prɔpɔntidat·rukɛmwɛ   pontikum sinum.

From CATULLUS.

Note that the distinguishing accents of long and short *i*
and *u* are not shown in the second extract. The differences
normally follow the quantity of the vowels, and the accents
are therefore hardly necessary.

The two extracts should be carefully studied.

Passages from Cicero, Horace and Catullus, with the
pronunciation carefully marked, are given by Professor
Feyerabend in his Latin-English Dictionary (pp. xiii—xvi).
The passages are not, however, reproduced here, as Professor
Feyerabend's method of syllable division is now hardly
acceptable.

CHAPTER XVI

A Chapter for Young Teachers

THE PHRASING OF LATIN WORDS FOR READING

As in English, so in Latin: correct phrasing depends upon a correct logical sentence-analysis. This does not mean the detailed grammatical analysis we teach in a Third Form English lesson, but rather a mere division into subject and predicate, with the various modifiers (qualifiers) of these set out in their relative degrees of subordination. With well-constructed English sentences of ordinary length, such an analysis is not necessary even for a Middle Form boy. He sees ahead sufficiently to be able to phrase his words intelligently. But in a long loose sentence, even a practised reader may find it difficult, without at least a first quick mental analysis, to catch the drift of the sentence as a whole and see how the parts hang together.

Here is such a sentence from Matthew Arnold (*Essays in Criticism*, Vol. I, p. 225). It is not a good sentence, but it serves as a good illustration. It is much too long drawn-out, and its completion is unduly suspended:

"The Passion Play at Ammergau, with its immense audiences, the seriousness of its actors, the passionate emotion of its spectators, brought to my mind something of which I had read an account lately; something produced, not in Bavaria nor in Christendom at all, but far away in that wonderful East, from which, whatever airs of superiority Europe may justly give itself, all our religion has come, and where religion,

of some sort or other, has still an empire over men's feelings
such as it has nowhere else."

Here is a useful logical analysis of the sentence:

A first skeleton:

Subject	Predicate	
The **Play**	brought to my mind	something

The skeleton may now be partly filled in, the various modifiers,
whether words, phrases, or clauses, being attached to their
principals (a few words are omitted, to save space):

Subject	Predicate	
The **Passion Play** 1. at Ammergau, 2. with its audiences, 3. the seriousness, 4. the emotion	brought to my mind	**something** 1. of which I had read an account, 2. produced (*a*) not in Bavaria or Christendom, but (*b*) in the East

The remainder of the sentence is a complex modifier
attached to the last word *East*, consisting of two subordinate
clauses, each with its own subordinate clause:

> the **East**
>
> > 1. *from which* our religion has come,
> >   whatever airs Europe may give itself,
> > 2. *where* religion has still an empire,
> >   such as it has nowhere else.

Although such an analysis is rarely required in English, it is the *sort* of analysis which a teacher of Latin often finds it an advantage to provide for boys who are beginning to read prose authors.

A word-to-word Latin construe should be ruled out of court entirely. Teach the boy to fasten on the Latin *phrase*, the word-*group*, it may be a subject with one or more simple modifiers, it may be an oblique case with its modifiers, it may be some form of absolute construction, it may be a whole subordinate clause, though if this clause is long it would naturally be broken up into one or more sub-groups of related words. And so on. The words of the phrase to be grouped are almost always closely related *grammatically*. Let successive co-ordinations be kept in parallel, and let successive sub-ordinations be sheered off more and more to the right, so that the learner sees not only the words in their natural groups, but the relations of the groups to one another. Not only does such an analysis provide a rational phrasing for reading, but translating into English becomes a really simple matter.

We may now give a logical analysis of one or two Latin sentences.

1. Gallia est omnis diuisa in partes tres, quarum unam incolunt Belgae, aliam Aquitani, tertiam, qui ipsorum lingua Celtae, nostra Galli, appellantur. Horum omnium fortissimi sunt Belgae, propterea quod a cultu atque humanitate prouinciae longissime absunt, minimeque ad eos mercatores saepe commeant, atque ea, quae ad effeminandos animos pertinent, important, proximique sunt Germanis, qui trans Rhenum incolunt, quibuscum continenter bellum gerunt. Qua de causa Heluetii quoque reliquos Gallos uirtute praece-

dunt, quod fere cottidianis proeliis cum Germanis contendunt, cum aut suis finibus eos prohibent aut ipsi in eorum finibus bellum gerunt. (*De Bello Gallico*, I.)

For beginners some modification of word order is quite permissible in a first analysis, and contracted sentences may be filled in :

> Gallia omnis diuisa est in partes tres,
>
> > **quarum,**
> >
> > > 1. Belgae unam incolunt
> > > 2. Aquitani aliam „
> > > 3. Celtae ⎫
> > >   *or* ⎬ tertiam „
> > >   Galli ⎭
> > >
> > > > viz., qui *ipsorum* lingua Celtae appellantur
> > > >   „ *nostra* „ Galli „
>
> Horum omnium, fortissimi sunt Belgae,
>
> > **propterea quod**
> >
> > > 1. a cultu atque human. prou. long. absunt, et minime mercatores
> > >
> > > > (*a*) ad eos saepe commeant, atque
> > > > (*b*) ea, quae ad effem. anim. pert., important;
> > >
> > > 2. proximique sunt Germanis,
> > >
> > > > (*a*) qui trans Rhenum incolunt,
> > > > (*b*) quibuscum continenter bellum gerunt.
>
> **Qua de causa,** Helu. quoque rel. Gall. uir. praecedunt,
>
> > **quod,** fere cottidianis proel. cum G. contendunt,
> >
> > > **cum,** 1. aut suis finibus eos prohibent,
> > >
> > > > 2. aut ipsi in eorum finibus bell. gerunt.

2. Noui enim moderationem animi tui et aequitatem, teque non cognomen solum Athenis deportasse, sed humanitatem et prudentiam intellego. et tamen te suspicor isdem rebus quibus me ipsum interdum grauius commoueri, quarum consolatio et maior est et in aliud tempus differenda. nunc autem uisum est mihi de senectute aliquid ad te conscribere. hoc enim onere, quod mihi commune tecum est, aut iam urgentis aut certe aduentantis senectutis et te et me ipsum leuari uolo. (*De Senectute.*)

Noui moderationem et aequitatem animi tui,
Intellego te deportasse, Athenis,
     non cognomen solum,
     sed humanitatem et prudentiam.
Suspicor te, interdum grauius, commoueri,
     iisdem rebus,
     quibus me ipsum;
          quarum consolatio
             maior est
             et in aliud tempus differenda.
Uisum est mihi, de senectute aliquid, ad te conscribere.
Uolo et te et me ipsum leuari
     hoc onere, quod mihi tecum commune est,
         ↓
senectutis, aut iam urgentis, aut certe aduentantis

This kind of help is legitimate at first: it is legitimate now and then even in Form VI where a specially difficult or obscure sentence is under consideration. But such props should be withdrawn as quickly as possible. The boy must learn to phrase for himself, and this will soon come if his teacher is consistent in his own phrasing.

3. Lastly we give a suitable logical analysis of a few
familiar lines from the *Æneid* (VII, 376—387):

> Tum uero infelix,
>> excita ingentibus monstris,
>> lymphata sine more,
>>> per urbem immensam, furit.
>
> Ceu quondam turbo,
>> sub uerbere torto uolitans,
>> quem pueri,
>>> intenti ludo,
>>> in gyro magno, circum atria uacua,
>>> exercent;
>
> Ille, actus habena, curuatis spatiis fertur.
>
> Manus impuber,
>> mirata buxum uolubile,
>> inscia supra,
>> stupet.
>
> Animos plagae dant.
>
> Agitur, illo, cursu non segnior,
>> per medias urbes, populosque feroces.
>
> Quin etiam in siluas euolat,
>> simulato numine Bacchi,
>> maius nefas adorta,
>> maioremque furorem orsa.
>
> Natum frondosis montibus abdit.

How far is verse-analysis, even of this simple kind, legitimate'? The poet hates the logician and all his ways. But
how can boys discover what the poet meant unless they are
taught to apply their reason to what he said? Anyhow, when
a boy begins his Virgil or his Horace, there is general agree-

ment that understanding of the meaning *must* precede any appreciation of the music; in other words, translation must precede a study of scansion. But once the boy is familiar with the form of the verse, scansion should begin to precede translation. Scansion helps phrasing enormously, and by its means verse falls into a sort of rational phrasing far more easily than prose does.

There is, of course, a rhythm in Latin prose, especially Cicero's prose, and it can often be felt at the end of sentences. But not all scholars seem to be able to catch the music of it. But no matter. Correct phrasing is the very essence of reading Latin aloud. Make pupils read plenty of Latin aloud, both prose and verse. Make them learn passages from Cicero by heart and recite them aloud. That way lies reward.

CHAPTER XVII

ANCIENT WRITERS' REFERENCES TO GREEK AND LATIN ACCENT

1. DIONYSIUS of Halicarnassus (circa B.C. 20) *de Comp.* 11.

Μουσικὴ γάρ τις ἦν καὶ ἡ τῶν πολιτικῶν λόγων ἐπιστήμη τῷ ποσῷ διαλλάττουσα τῆς ἐν ᾠδαῖς καὶ ὀργάνοις οὐχὶ τῶ ποιῷ....διαλέκτου μὲν οὖν μέλος ἑνὶ μετρεῖται διαστήματι τῷ λεγομένῳ διὰ πέντε ὡς ἔγγιστα· καὶ οὔτε ἐπιτείνεται πέρα τῶν τριῶν τόνων καὶ ἡμιτονίου ἐπὶ τὸ ὀξὺ[1] οὔτε ἀνίεται τοῦ χωρίου τούτου πλεῖον ἐπὶ τὸ βαρύ. οὐ μὴν ἅπασά γε ἡ λέξις ἡ καθ᾽ ἓν μόριον λόγου ταττομένη ἐπὶ τῆς αὐτῆς λέγεται

[1] " Rises in pitch of 3 tones and a half (the measure of a Fifth in the musical scale)" (Ellis).

τάσεως· ἀλλ᾽ ἡ μὲν ἐπὶ τῆς ὀξείας, ἡ δὲ ἐπὶ τῆς βαρείας, ἡ δὲ
ἐπ᾽ ἀμφοῖν. τῶν δὲ ἀμφοτέρας τὰς τάσεις ἐχουσῶν αἱ μὲν
κατὰ μίαν συλλαβὴν συνεφθαρμένον ἔχουσι τῷ ὀξεῖ τὸ
βαρύ, ἃς δὴ περισπωμένας καλοῦμεν· αἱ δὲ ἐν ἑτέρᾳ τε καὶ
ἑτέρᾳ χωρὶς ἑκάτερον, ἐφ᾽ ἑαυτοῦ τὴν οἰκείαν φυλάττον φύσιν·
καὶ ταῖς μὲν δισυλλάβοις οὐδὲν τὸ διὰ μέσου χωρίον βαρύτη-
τός τε καὶ ὀξύτητος· ταῖς δὲ πολυσυλλάβοις ἡλίκαι ποτ᾽ ἂν
ὦσιν ἡ τὸν ὀξὺν τόνον ἔχουσα μία ἐν πολλαῖς ταῖς ἄλλαις
βαρείαις ἔνεστιν. ἡ δὲ ὀργανική τε καὶ ᾠδικὴ μοῦσα διαστή-
μασί τε χρῆται πλείοσιν οὐ τῷ διὰ πέντε μόνον, ἀλλ᾽ ἀπὸ
τοῦ διὰ πασῶν¹ ἀρξαμένη καὶ τὸ διὰ πέντε μελῳδεῖ καὶ τὸ
διὰ τεσσάρων καὶ τὸ διάτονον καὶ τὸ ἡμιτόνιον, ὡς δέ τινες
οἴονται, καὶ τὴν δίεσιν αἰσθητῶς.

¹ "An Octave...a Fifth...a Fourth...a Tone...a Semitone...a Quarter
Tone" (id.).

2. VITRUVIUS (circa B.C. 20) *de archit.* V 4 2 (based on Aristoxenus).

Vox enim mutationibus cum flectitur, alias fit acuta,
alias grauis, duobusque modis mouetur e quibus unus effectus
habet continuatos¹, alter distantes². continuata uox neque
in finitionibus consistit neque in loco ullo³, efficitque termi-
nationes non apparentes, interualla autem media apparentia,
uti sermone cum dicamus *sol, lux, flos, uox.* nunc enim nec
unde incipit nec ubi desinit intellegitur, nec quae
ex acuta facta est grauis, ex graui acuta apparet auribus.
per distantiam autem e contrario. namque cum flectitur

¹ =συνεχής (κίνησις) Aristox. (12, 3 M.).   ² διαστηματική, *id.*   ³ Cf. Aristox.
κατὰ μὲν οὖν τὴν συνεχῆ (κίνησιν) τόπον τινὰ διεξιέναι φαίνεται ἡ φωνὴ τῇ αἰσθήσει
οὕτως ὡς ἂν μηδαμῶς ἱσταμένη μηδ᾽ ἐπ᾽ αὐτῶν τῶν περάτων κατά γε τὴν τῆς
αἰσθήσεως φαντασίαν, ἀλλὰ φερομένη συνεχῶς μέχρι σιωπῆς.

inmutatione uox, statuit se in alicuius sonitus finitionem, deinde in alterius[1] et id ultro citro crebre faciendo inconstans apparet sensibus, uti in cantionibus, cum flectentes uocem uarietatem facimus modulationis.

[1] Aristox. διαβαίνουσα (ἡ φωνή) ἵστησιν αὐτὴν ἐπὶ μιᾶς τάσεως, εἶτα πάλιν ἐφ᾽ ἑτέρας, καὶ τοῦτο ποιοῦσα συνεχῶς—λέγω δὲ συνεχῶς κατὰ τὸν χρόνον—ὑπερ-βαίνουσα μὲν τοὺς περιεχομένους ὑπὸ τῶν τάσεων τόπους, ἱσταμένη δ᾽ ἐπ᾽ αὐτῶν τῶν τάσεων καὶ φθεγγομένη ταύτας μόνον αὐτὰς μελωδεῖν λέγεται καὶ κινεῖσθαι διαστηματικὴν κίνησιν.

3. CICERO, *Orator* (B.C. 46) § 58.

ipsa enim natura, quasi modularetur hominum oratio-nem, in omni uerbo posuit acutam uocem nec una plus nec a postrema syllaba citra tertiam.

4. QUINTILIAN (circa A.D. 90), *Inst. Or.* I 5 30, 31.

Namque in omni uoce acuta intra numerum trium syllabarum continetur, siue eae sunt in uerbo solae siue ultimae et in iis aut proxima extremae aut ab ea tertia. trium porro de quibus loquor media longa aut acuta aut flexa erit; eodem loco breuis utique grauem habebit sonum, ideo-que positam ante se id est ab ultima tertiam acuet. est autem in omni uoce utique acuta sed numquam plus una nec umquam ultima ideoque in disyllabis prior; praeterea numquam in eadem flexa et acuta. itaque neutra cludet uocem Latinam, ea uero quae sunt syllabae unius, erunt acuta aut flexa ne sit aliqua uox sine acuta.

5. *id.* XII 10 33.

Accentus quoque cum rigore quodam, tum similitudine ipsa minus suaues (sc. quam Graeci) habemus, quia ultima syllaba nec acuta umquam excitatur nec flexa circumducitur, sed in grauem aut duas grauis cadit semper. itaque tanto est sermo Graecus Latino iucundior, ut nostri poetae, quotiens dulce carmen esse uoluerunt, illorum id nominibus exornent.

6. *id.* I 5 28.

Euenit ut metri quoque condicio mutet accentum, *pecudes pictaeque uolucres:* nam *uolúcres* media acuta legam quia, etsi natura breuis, tamen positione longa est, ne faciat iambum, quem non recipit uersus herous.

7. *id.* I 5 25 sqq.

Ceterum scio iam quosdam eruditos nonnullos etiam grammaticos sic docere ac loqui ut propter quaedam uocum discrimina uerbum interim acuto sono finiant, ut in illis *quae circúm litora, circúm Piscosos scopulos* ne, si grauem posuerint secundam, *círcus* dici uideatur non *circuitus.* itemque cum *quale* interrogantes graui, comparantes acuto tenore pronuntiant quod tamen in aduerbiis fere solis ac pronominibus uindicant, in ceteris ueterem legem sequuntur. mihi uidetur condicionem mutare quod his locis uerba coniungimus. nam cum dico *circum lítora* tamquam unum enuntio dissimulata distinctione, itaque tamquam in una uoce una est acuta, quod idem accidit in illo *Troiae qui primus ab óris.*

APPENDIX

From the plaint of a scholarly rimester of a century ago[1]

"So great the evil has been left to grow,
That scarce a Roman now his name would know
At Oxford or at Cambridge; scarce a word,
As now pronounced, at Rome was ever heard.
In good old times, before the world ran mad,
Latin the same pronunciation had
Through all the earth : it differs now among
The several peoples as each mother tongue.
  Is there a boy that thumbs his Valpian leaves—
A blockhead whom the fallacy deceives ?
Does not the urchin blest with half a *brain know*
That Virgil never said *virumque cano ?*
Try any modern tongue, 'twill not submit
To any sound that not belongs to it :
How would our Alma Mater hiss and *hoot,*
Should any poet make his grave *debut,*
With such a rhyme ! but mightily will *please her*
Horatian courtiers coupling thus their *Cæsar.*
Yet this than that a better rhyme *is not,*
Nor were it worse to couple thus *Guizot,*
(For either you must mispronounce the word
Or to the rhyme the error is transferred ;)

---

[1] These lines are from a book by an anonymous scholar, published by William Brittain, 54 Paternoster Row. It was called *Living Latin.* The rhymes dealt minutely with the different speech sounds of Latin and with the difficulties of Latin accent, and many authorities were quoted. The rules laid down are naturally not all in accord with the results of the researches of the last fifty years, but the book is a lively protest against the slipshod method of reading Latin at that time.

Go, then, to ancient Rome, to Paris go,
And learn the names of Cæsar and Guizot.

 Sirs, 'tis high time it should at length be stopt,
The barbarous reading which we now adopt,
Missounding every syllable, misplacing
Their time and accent, and the whole defacing.

 Their tuneful cadence cannot be discerned
When dactyls into anapests are turned,
And leaping anapests their lofty bound
Change for a dactyl canter on the ground;
Or when iambics volatile and gay
Like soft trochaics gently march away:
The time's destroyed when long for short may pass,
And short for long,—in one chaotic mass,
Void of all order, harmony and rule,
As Anarchy himself might ridicule.

. . . .

Our masters taught us this (they taught us wrong)—
To give the sounds to Latin which belong
To English: very well; but stop and see
How English with itself doth disagree.
So multi-toned is English, and in its
Orthoepy such various sounds admits,
That there is scarce a tongue on earth unable
To find its likeness in the modern Babel.
What English sound, then, shall we choose for Latin?
(I speak now of the A,) shall it be that in
Fat, father, fade, or what, or all, or any?
Think you the Latin letters had as many
Varieties of sound? *they had but one,*
Lengthened or shortened, and beside it none."

. . . .

BIBLIOGRAPHY

1. Handbook of Phonetics. H. Sweet. Oxford, 1877.
2. Primer of Phonetics. H. Sweet. Oxford, 1906.
3. Elements of Phonetics. W. Rippmann. London, 1899.
4. Elemente der Phonetik. W. Vietor. Leipsic, 1904.
5. Lehrbuch der Phonetik. O. Jespersen. Leipsic, 1904.
6. Petite Phonétique. Paul Passy. Leipsic, 1912.
7. Le Maître Phonétique, Mai—Juin 1911. (Pp. 80—81, Chinese "tones"; by Daniel Jones.)
8. Early English pronunciation. A. J. Ellis. London, 1869.
9. Visible Speech. Bell. London, 1867.
10. Outlines of Latin Phonetics. Niedermann. Translation by Strong and Stewart. London, 1910.
11. Quantitative pronunciation of Latin. A. J. Ellis. London, 1874.
12. The Roman pronunciation of Latin. J. B. Scheier. Notre Dame, Indiana, 1894.
13. The Roman pronunciation of Latin. F. E. Lord. Boston, U.S.A., 1895.
14. Pronunciation of Latin in the Augustan period. Camb. Phil. Soc., 1905.
15. Restored pronunciation of Greek and Latin. Arnold and Conway. Cambridge, 1906.
16. How to pronounce Latin. J. P. Postgate. London, 1907.
17. Théorie générale de l'Accentuation Latine. Weil et Benloew. Paris, 1855.
18. Petit Traité de Prononciation Latine. A. Bos. Paris, 1893.
19. Livre de Lecture Latine. A. Bos. Paris, 1897.
20. Traité Élémentaire de Prononciation Latine. Aristide Sécheresse. Paris, 1903.

21. Aussprache, Vokalismus und Betonung der lateinischen Sprache (2 vols.). Corssen. Leipsic, 1870.
22. Die Aussprache des Latein. Emil Seelmann. Heilbronn, 1885.
23. Hülfsbüchlein für die Aussprache der lateinischen Vokale in positionslangen Silben. Anton Marx. Berlin. (Last edition, 1901, now a good deal out of date.)
24. Lautlehre der lateinischen Sprache. F. Stolz. Leipsic, 1894.
25. Handbuch der lateinischen Laut- und Formenlehre. F. Sommer. Heidelberg, 1902.
26. Grammatici Latini, ed. Keil. Leipsic, 1855—1880.
27. Grundriss der Romanischen Philologie. Gröber. Strassburg, 1888 ff.
28. The Latin Language. W. M. Lindsay. Oxford, 1894.
29. The Latin Language, especially pp. 36—72, on hidden quantities. C. E. Bennett. Boston, U.S.A., 1907.
30. Latin Grammar, Part I. Roby. London.
31. School Latin Grammar. Roby. London.
32. Public School Latin Grammar. Kennedy. London.
33. The New Latin Primer. J. P. Postgate and C. A. Vince. London.
34. Latin Grammar. Hale and Buck. Boston, U.S.A., 1903.
35. Grundriss der vergleichenden Grammatik. K. Brugmann. Leipsic. Vol. I, 1897.
36. Ausführliche Grammatik der lateinischen Sprache (2 vols.). New Edition. Kühner. Hanover.
37. Précis de grammaire comparée du Grec et du Latin. Victor Henry. Paris, 1894.
38. Grammaire comparée du Grec et du Latin, Vol. I. O. Riemann et H. Goelzer. Paris, 1897.
39. Manual of Latin Prosody. (Seventh edition.) W. Ramsay. London.
40. Traité de Versification Latine. L. Quicherat. Paris, 1882.
41. Nouvelle Prosodie Latine. L. Quicherat. Paris, 1903.
42. De re Metrica. L. Mueller. St Petersburg and Leipsic. 1894.
43. Corpus Inscriptionum Latinarum. Berlin, 1863 ff.
44. A Latin Dictionary for Schools. Lewis. Oxford, 1901. (Better than Lewis and Short for hidden quantities.)

45. Lateinisch-Deutsches Schul- und Handwörterbuch. Stowasser. Leipsic, 1910.
46. Latin-English Dictionary. K. Feyerabend. Berlin, 1912.
47. Kleines Lateinisch-Deutsches Schulwörterbuch. Heinichen; revised by Blase and Reeb. Leipsic, 1911.
48. Classical Review, Vol. XIII, 1899, Review of Brugmann's Comparative Grammar. J. P. Postgate.
49. Classical Review, Vol. XIX, 1905, "Vendryes, and the Ancients, on Greek Accents." J. P. Postgate.
50. Journal of the British Academy, Vol. III, 1908, "Flaws in Classical Research." J. P. Postgate.
51. Classical Philology, Vol. I, No. 1, "Latin syllabification: evidence of inscriptions." Walter Dennison.
52. Classical Philology, Vol III, No. 1, "Accent in Latin." J. P. Postgate.
53. Hermathena, 1908, "'Sprechtempo' or Phonetic Law?" C. Exon.
54 Papers on Hidden Quantities. See p. 59, footnote. Professor Buck's paper in the Classical Review for June 1913 is of special interest. Professor Sonnenschein writes a short final reply in the Classical Review for August 1913. See also vol. 29, *supra*.

Lightning Source UK Ltd.
Milton Keynes UK
UKOW04f0435080415

249286UK00001B/11/P